I0569192

BRANDON MILES

# Suburban Addict

*A Lifeline for Addicts and Those Who Love Them*

*First published by Suburban Addict 2025*

*Copyright © 2025 by Brandon Miles*

*All rights reserved. No part of this publication may be reproduced, stored or transmitted in any form or by any means, electronic, mechanical, photocopying, recording, scanning, or otherwise without written permission from the publisher. It is illegal to copy this book, post it to a website, or distribute it by any other means without permission.*

*First edition*

*ISBN: 979-8-218-60745-6*

*This book was professionally typeset on Reedsy.*
*Find out more at reedsy.com*

*To Dad,*
*For the loving anchor you were,*
*And color you brought to each moment.*

*To Mom,*
*For the real life angel you are,*
*and endless love that defines you.*

*To Rye,*
*For your genuine care,*
*and guiding light in this life.*

Just once in my life I cried tears of joy. It was while contemplating if my life was worth saving.

I realized that should I die, so would my family. Every day, for the remainder of their days.

This moment changed the course of everything.

# Contents

# Preface

For a long time, I struggled with how to start this book. The last thing I wanted was for it to come off as some endless string of advice or profound thoughts. Let's be real—most of us barely practice half the wisdom we hear, and that's exactly the point. This journey, for you and your family, is going to require a daily choice to move forward. Some days, that choice won't feel consistent or even possible, and that's okay. That's just reality. I'll admit, I worried that my story might not seem as raw or intense as others, but the truth is, my story is probably the most common of all. And if there's one thing I hope you take from this book, it's not just a sense of connection but the realization that without change, things can—and will—get worse.

Years ago, I lost everything I'd written with my laptop. Every word, every thought poured out over years, gone in an instant. It was devastating. That loss came alongside waves of other heartbreaks. I lost my father. I lost most of my money in the market. The hits just kept coming. And in those moments I had a choice: I could dwell on the past, letting it shape my future, or I could let go and see what life had in store next.

It's easy to get caught up in the chaos of everything happening around us. It feels like fighting against waves, and sooner or later, resistance becomes your whole world. To surrender though, and ride the process out to an opening? That's some-thing entirely different.

# Prologue

*The most important aspect when dealing with an addiction of any type is that there is a lesson in why we are currently experiencing this challenge. All addictions initially serve a purpose—helping us feel better about ourselves than we currently do. The addiction helps us get through what seems to be an impossible time in our lives. It allows us to avoid feeling the fear of thinking we are not powerful and unlimited.*

*The second important aspect of living through an addiction is that it allows us to discover our inner power. When we can pull ourselves out of the darkness and find the light, that is when we truly experience a love and empowerment for ourselves that screams, "I can be, do, and have anything! I am the power and the light!" This level of empowerment helps us remember that happiness, self-love, self-empowerment, and self-awareness come from within—never from an outside source.*

*When we let go of the false beliefs learned from our parents, elders, friends, or society, our sense of self-worth assists us in overcoming the need to continue the addiction.*

*Our false sense of emptiness triggers the need for addiction to make us feel fulfilled. However, the truth of who you are only knows that you are perfect and unconditionally loved. Therefore, when we allow ourselves to become the source of our love, we will naturally feel fulfilled. This sense of inner love will overpower the need for addiction. You are the answer. You are the healer!*

Dr. Matt Singer

# Introduction

When I think about the experiences you're about to read, I get that same gut-check feeling you get before dropping bad news on someone you care about. You know, the "Is this really a good idea? How's this going to go over? Maybe I should just keep it to myself" kind of feeling. And trust me, keeping it all locked up feels like the easier choice most of the time.

But here's the thing: there's incredible power in the truth. It's a force that can keep us from walking straight into the kind of mistakes we only learn to regret the hard way. Over the years, I've seen that the more you lie—to yourself, to others—the closer you get to hitting rock bottom. Truth doesn't just show you opportunities; it holds you accountable. It makes you own what you're putting into the game. So while I'm not expecting this book to change everyone who reads it, I can promise you this:

The lives we lead will always come down to our choices. Choices become habits, habits shape emotions, and those emotions steer the course of our lives. If you want to change your emotions, you've got to make new choices—choices that align with who you are and who you want to be. Keep making the same choices, and you'll stay stuck in the same old ruts. But commit to new ones, and you'll discover the kind of life you've always wanted.

Now, if you're reading this because someone close to you is battling addiction, chances are you don't fully understand what they're going through. That's okay. This book is here to lay it all out: how an addict thinks, what you can do to help, and what you can't. Here's the first truth you need to hear: this isn't your burden to fix. You can't save them, and you shouldn't beat yourself up over that. The only person who can make real change is the addict themselves.

And to the addicts out there: if you're still stuck in this mess and blaming everyone but yourself, it's time for a reality check. At the end of the day, you're your own solution. The principles you choose to live by—or not—are entirely up to you.

## A Light

During one of the darkest years of my addiction, I attended a weekend-long workshop in New York City. It wasn't specifically about addiction; it was designed to help people peel back the layers of their programmed thinking and get to the core of who they really are. Over two hundred of us gathered in one room, digging deep into our lives. For a moment, the workshop helped you see through all the bullshit life piles on—the defenses, the habits, the lies you tell yourself. It was raw, emotional, and transformational.

When the breakthroughs came, you were invited to share your experience with the group—a chance to connect with others and perhaps even impact their lives. I'd had a few profound experiences before then. Experiences you could only assume came from something divine, something bigger than everyone in the room. We might not have been aware of it immediately, but there was an energy present, and it showed itself through special moments and interactions.

Over the weekend, I shared my story of addiction with many people. Some were drawn to it, while others listened politely and moved on. One moment stood out. I was talking in a circle when I noticed an older woman standing nearby, quietly observing. After the conversation ended, we were called back to our seats. As I sat down, I felt a hand on mine. I looked up, and it was her. Tears filled her eyes, and there was a warmth in her presence that I can't fully describe.

She reached out with her other hand and placed a small folded piece of paper in mine. "I don't know why I'm doing this," she said softly. "I'm a very introverted person, but something is telling me to. I'm a nurse here in New York, and I've had to wrap the bodies of so many young people who've died from addiction. I've had to speak to their parents, cry with them... and hearing your story hurt me all the same. I want you to promise me something: promise me you're going to stay alive. Live a full life. Don't let this addiction win."

As she spoke, tears poured down my face. I nodded, unable to say anything. She let go of my hand, turned, and returned to her seat. When I unfolded the paper, it simply read, "Brandon = Wellness." I've kept it with me to this day.

The weekend continued, and I began to realize that we were all there for the same reason: to understand each other's journeys.

At the core of it, we all wanted the same things—connection, understanding, and happiness. On the final day, I sat in the back of the room, listening as others shared their epiphanies, wondering why mine hadn't come yet. Next to me was a girl from my smaller group. Her story was heartbreaking—one of childhood abuse and neglect. She had spent years avoiding all human touch. For her, affection wasn't just undesirable; it felt completely out of reach. An hour later, I sat in the same corner, face in my hands, eyes closed, waiting for clarity. And then it hit me. Maybe it was a meditative state or just the culmination of everything I'd experienced that weekend, but my realization came. I thought back to the old woman and her words: did I truly want to live? For the first time, I forced myself to confront the question. The answer wasn't clear, and that scared me.

Then, a deeper truth emerged: if I were to die, it wouldn't just be my end. My family would suffer every day from the pain I'd leave behind. That realization broke me open. Tears flowed, but this time, they weren't from sadness—they were from joy. For the first time, I felt a reason to live. Suddenly, I felt arms wrap around me. It was the girl from my group! The one who avoided all touch. She didn't know why I was crying so hard, but something in that moment moved her to overcome her own barriers. It was a series of such synchronized moments, I still have a hard time believing it ever happened.

Honoring the process, I walked to the front of the room to share my experience. Mind you this was in front of two hundred people, most of whom I had never met or known before that weekend. As I spoke to the crowd I could see tears run down faces, with a tangible energy you could feel only being there. At the end of the day, there were a number of people that came to me in awe for what I had shared. One man in particular approached and introduced himself. He told me his story and reason for attendance; that he hadn't spoken to his oldest son in ten years, and all because of a family feud. He went on to say that because of my willingness to share with the group, he was moved to call his son. They had made plans to see each other that next week for the first time in a decade.

I'll never fully understand what happened over those few days. The timing, the connections—it all felt like it came from another place. For a brief moment, there was light, purpose, meaning, and it was just enough to ignite change.

# THE BEGINNING

"Knowing yourself is the beginning of all wisdom."
- Aristotle -

When did it start?

**N**o one sets out with the intention of becoming an addict. From my experience, it often begins in those vulnerable years of youth, when you're grappling with growing pains and a seemingly harmless drug sneaks into your life. At first, it feels like a friend—one that promises to take the edge off any pain or struggle life throws your way. But here's the kicker: pain, as overwhelming as it feels when you're young, is a necessary ingredient for growth.

Every young person faces their own challenges, from minor inconveniences to life-shaking events. But for addicts, those challenges morph into something more insidious. Addiction stunts your growth, halting your journey to becoming the person you want to be. Take me, for example: I've always been terrified of public speaking. Not just nervous—terrified. The mere thought of standing in front of a crowd would spiral into "What if I say something stupid? What if I have a panic attack?" That fear led me to avoid it at all costs. Once, I even took a full letter-grade deduction in college just to dodge presenting my final paper. That's where addiction crept in. Instead of facing my fear, I retreated to the false comfort drugs provided, convincing myself everything was fine—even great.

This is the crux of the problem for addicts: they view their challenges not as opportunities for growth but as failures to be avoided. They're stuck in a loop of avoidance, dodging discomfort and, in doing so, missing the stepping stones to a better future. For me, that avoidance came at the cost of progress, leaving me stuck in the same cycle of pain and setback.

Here's the truth most addicts don't want to face: avoiding pain doesn't eliminate it. It only lets it fester until it becomes unbearable. This is especially true in today's world of endless social comparison, where discomfort feels like a flaw rather than a part of the process. So, what do addicts do? They avoid. They avoid until avoidance is no longer an option.

The hardest part to look back on, beyond where it all began, is the point where it gained momentum. For most, drug use starts as an occasional escape—a "few and far between" kind of thing. But over time, it snowballs. Once in a while turns into every other weekend, then every weekend, then weekdays. Eventually, a barrier is broken, and what began as a casual indulgence becomes an unshakable necessity.

## First Time

The first try might be one of the sweetest, most love-filled, blanketing moments you can experience. At the time, nothing comes close to it, and nothing ever will. Like one of your first happy memories as a child, every emotion fades away and is replaced with an overwhelming sense of love and warmth. Everything you experience in that moment feels more amazing than it ever has. Suddenly, you're in a state of complete optimism about life and all its challenges. In fact, those challenges almost seem enjoyable to think about. The moment itself feels like something you never want to end, and you're already contemplating the next use. From this point on, no other experience can compete. And while you're blissfully unaware of the problems ahead, you don't care because it's erased all the ones in the present.

For some, that first experience turns out to be their last. But for others, it's only the beginning. They might go through a first-time sickness, but that discomfort pales in comparison to the growing desire for a repeat experience. Worst of all, they have no idea what purpose this drug is starting to serve. They've fallen through a trap door that leads to others—each with harder falls and steeper climbs back to the surface. And no one is there to warn them of what's to come.

## First Week

It takes time to build up to daily use, but eventually, you reach a point where you've gone several days in a row and think, "Wow, I should probably stop and take a break." Let's say you do take that break. You've now set a personal boundary, your own ceiling—for now. But over time, that ceiling becomes the new floor. You'll push it a few times, maybe even stick to your planned breaks, thinking you've got it all under control. But then you start stretching the pattern—a few more days of consecutive use here and there. Before you know it, you've used for a week straight. It's alarming, but everything still seems okay.

Somewhere along the way, you start noticing how much relief it provides from the stress of your weekdays. What a comfort to know that no matter how hard things get, you have something to wash it all away. But what you don't realize is that with every cycle, the stress and anxiety are actually growing stronger. Not because they've changed, but because you've grown weaker.

If only you knew how life-altering these decisions would be. Choices that seem to erase your struggles and pain in the moment, only to pave the way for something much worse: addiction.

## First Month

Four weeks in, the conscious version of "you"—the one that existed before you started using—is still very much alive. It's keeping you anchored, with no real concern about losing your grip on reality. But you're starting to notice little things. The balance in your checking account isn't what it used to be. Going out doesn't seem as fun anymore. And no matter what you're doing, you're constantly imagining how much better it would be if you were high.

Once a week, you toy with the idea of stopping. You recognize the gravity of the situation but underestimate the power addiction has already begun to hold over you. Sure, you could stop cold turkey (anyone can, right?), but separating yourself from this growing pattern is harder than you'd like to admit. The longer you wait, the harder it becomes.

At this point, it's only been one month. One month of use against an entire lifetime of normalcy. You still have the strength to take control—to regain the part of you that's slipping away. But time is running out. Drug use doesn't just make you weaker to life's challenges; it amplifies the weaknesses you already had. If you're serious about stopping, you need more than just a vague plan. You need a clear strategy. Identify your vulnerabilities and face them head-on, no matter the cost or embarrassment. This is your life on the line, and it could be your last chance to turn back.

## First Year

365 days in, reality begins to set in. You fully recognize there's a problem, but the drug is serving you so well that it outweighs any desire to address it. You keep going, blocking out your conscience and pushing the gas pedal harder. In your mind, you're young, and taking risks feels like living. Better yet, you tell yourself you have years ahead to figure this out. The thought of being in this same mess five or ten years from now would shock you, but you're not calculating the time you're losing— time you'll need to rebuild. Meanwhile, your boat has left the dock, heading toward a horizon of uncertainty. You have no rudder, no oar, no sense of direction. Carried by the tide of an uncontrollable force, your ability to gain control feels out of reach. All you can do is hope and pray that something greater is at work.

Somewhere along the way, there's a moment of reconciliation— a brief recognition of the gap between who you are today and who you were a year ago. All this time, you've blurred the lines of that separation, using it as an anchor to the old you. Like a safe harbor you believe you'll return to, it blinds you to how far you've drifted. But at some point, you snap out of it and realize you're past the point of no return. Stopping now will require ten times the effort it would have before. Still, you're under the illusion that you can handle this on your own.

## First Denial

"I'm fine. I've always been fine. Nothing has ever steered me off course, so how could this?"

In part, I don't think anyone is to blame for their first moment of denial. It's not that you're naive; you're just human. If life is a game of mental warfare, and staying optimistic is part of survival, don't we owe it to ourselves to show strength in times of adversity? Our instinct isn't to ask for help, especially if we take pride in our independence.

So if denial worked the first time, why not use it again? The reason is simple: denial leads to a brick wall that reads, "I need help." When you finally hit that wall, tears fill your eyes as you wonder how you ever got here. The truth is too painful to face, so you take a glimpse, absorb the sting, and use it as an excuse to cope. A new pattern forms—one built on avoiding the truth.

## First Relapse

So you've decided to stop. You've put in the effort and mapped out a plan for success. The timeline is set, the schedule is organized, and expectations are aligned. Everything seems perfect—except for the expectations.

Where most people trip up is when reality doesn't match their expectations. When things don't go according to plan, you blame yourself for miscalculating. But maybe it's not about the perfect plan or flawless execution. Maybe it's about how you handle the plan's imperfections. It's not about having backup plans; it's about being prepared for failure and knowing you have a choice to make in those moments.

This is the mental battle of addiction—one that's often ignored. If the strength of your mind drove you to use in the first place, how can you expect to overcome addiction without addressing that same mind?

Looking back on my first relapse, I didn't recognize what was ahead beyond overcoming physical withdrawals. After that, I tried to take life head-on, and I failed. At the first sign of struggle, I realized that the reward of overcoming it wasn't enough to compete with the escape opiates offered. There was no alternative, no support system, and no one to share my emotions with. In that moment, and many moments after, I chose to relapse.

## First Acknowledgment

There are moments in life when that voice inside your head speaks up—clear, insistent, and impossible to ignore. It's like a guide, a warning light flashing louder and brighter each time you dismiss it. But eventually, you reach a breaking point. Maybe you got caught. Maybe guilt finally caught up with you. Or maybe the weight of your choices became too much to bear. Whatever the trigger, your decisions have created a narrative you can't live with anymore. You've ignored the signs for too long, and now you're paying the price. The only question left is: what are you going to do next?

At this crossroads, two paths usually emerge. Both are necessary in their own way, but neither will seem easy. The first is to confront your addiction privately, to try and fix it on your own, without letting anyone else in. The second is to open up—to share your struggles with family, friends, and the people who care about you.

Most of us will choose the first path at first. It feels safer. You want to believe you can handle it on your own because, after all, you're the one who got yourself into this mess. Why involve anyone else?

The truth is, involving others doesn't make you weaker—it makes you stronger. Accountability is a powerful tool. Sharing your addiction with those who love you is a risk, sure. It's vulnerable and terrifying. But the rewards—trust, relationships, health, happiness, security—are worth every ounce of fear.

Put the power back in your hands by making that first move. Don't let the discovery of your addiction be yet another consequence of it. Instead, take control by being the one to share your truth. Gain strength by revealing your weakness, and watch how it transforms not just you, but the people around you.

## First Last Time

Knowing the right time to stop often comes from trial and error. You've likely had attempts where you made it farther than expected and others where you fell flat on your face. The key to avoiding those crashes is learning to recognize the moments when you have the best shot at success. For instance, if you plan to quit on a Monday but know you're about to face a stressful week at work, maybe that's not the right time.

The hard truth is there's never a perfect time to stop. Any attempt—successful or not—is an achievement in itself. What matters most is what you take from each attempt. Each one is a stepping stone, raising the bar just a little higher. Even if you're not where you want to be, the effort creates patterns that will shape your future. Keep growing. Keep pushing. Every attempt builds momentum, even when it feels like you're standing still.

What drives most of us to that first last time is realizing we can't afford to lose any more. Maybe it's your health, your financial stability, or the relationships that addiction has eroded. Whatever it is, the pain of that loss becomes the catalyst for change.

At first, progress might feel slow—two steps forward, one step back. But over time, those small wins will start to connect. Block by block, a foundation takes shape. Then one day, you'll step back and realize you've built something solid. After knowing only loss and backpedaling for so long, this moment of clarity is relieving.

That first glimpse of progress brings something powerful: motivation. With it comes a shift—a new pattern fueled by self-belief. You'll keep moving forward, but you'll also carry an important lesson: failure is part of the process. Every stumble teaches you something. Every loss contains a gain, even if you can't see it yet.

So keep going. Your first last time is the beginning of something bigger.

**KEY TAKEAWAYS**

FOR THE ADDICTS:

**Give yourself grace.** Recovery takes time and space. Be patient with yourself as you navigate this journey.

**Failure is not defeat.** Your first attempt won't be perfect—and that's okay. Every stumble is a step closer to success.

**Think strategically, not emotionally.** Treat this like a game of chess. A misstep doesn't end the game; it just means adjusting your next move.

**Celebrate the first attempt.** Stopping, even for a moment, is a massive win. One day, you'll look back and see it as the beginning of change.

**Visualize the future.** No matter how long you've been using or what you've lost, there's always a path forward. Picture it. Believe in it.

**Put skin in the game.** Share your plans to stop with someone you trust. Accountability elevates commitment and builds support.

FOR FAMILY & LOVED ONES:

**Avoid confrontation.** If you sense something is wrong, don't try to "catch" them. Addiction thrives in shame, not trust.

**Observe quietly.** Monitor the situation with care, but avoid making them feel under surveillance.

**Create a safe space.** Conversations work better when they feel voluntary. Don't back them into a corner.

**Share your struggles.** Vulnerability can bridge the gap. Sharing your experience may encourage them to open up about theirs.

**Let go of control.** Their journey is theirs. Support them without trying to take over.

**Ask, don't demand.** Pose fair questions and suggest checkpoints for progress. Gentle guidance beats rigid ultimatums.

**Be relatable, not judgmental.** Empathize with their emotions and situation. Connection matters more than criticism.

# FRIENDS

"One friend in a storm is worth more than a thousand in
sunshine."
- Matshona Dhliwayo -

## Real Ones

One of the hardest parts of navigating addiction
is coming to terms with how much changes over
time. Friends, family, your environment—everything
evolves, while you, the addict, remain stuck. Addiction halts
your growth. Wherever you were when the drug use began,
that's where your maturity level pauses. Meanwhile, life moves
forward without you.

It's a painful realization when you finally notice how much
you've missed. Milestones, memories, relationships—lost
because you were too afraid to face the present. Too afraid to
cope with emotions without the crutch of escape. That's how it
starts: a handful of friends, a few shared highs. But over time,
those friends stop. They move on, grow up, and mature. And

you? You stay.

And when they express concern, it feels like judgment. "Who are they to lecture me?" you think. But let's be real: if they've moved on and you haven't, why wouldn't they worry?

Confronting an addict, though—it's a delicate, messy process. Our first reaction to criticism or concern is almost always defensive. We'll say whatever it takes to deflect, to shut it down. We might even flip the script, turning the microscope on them instead. That's unfair, but it's our way of protecting the addiction. We push away the people who care about us the most because they're the ones who see the truth. And the truth threatens our high.

Here's the thing: no one is responsible for your addiction—not your friends, not anyone else. The friends who tried to help, who cared enough to call you out, did so because they loved you. They remembered the person you were before all this started. They believed that person was still in there, buried but not gone.

Take a moment to think about the friends you've lost or pushed away because of your choices. Did you blame them? Did you tell yourself it was their fault—that they didn't understand, or that they somehow contributed to your problem? Check yourself. That blame doesn't belong to them. Even if they used with you in the beginning, they weren't the ones who kept you on this path. That was your choice.

It's easy to take friendships for granted when life is good. People surround you when times are easy; it doesn't take much to find company when the sun is shining. But the real ones? They're the ones who stick around when the sky is falling. They're the ones who don't flinch when your world is in pieces.

These are the friends who matter. The ones who cared enough to raise the red flag, even when it put them at risk of being pushed away. The ones who didn't let your defenses scare them off. Cherish them. Recognize their value. Because when the dust settles, and you finally take that step forward, it's the real ones who'll still be standing there, ready to help you rebuild.

## Partners In Crime

One of my closest friends called me at work one day to tell me he was checking into rehab. It hit me like a freight train. He was my partner in crime, the one I thought would somehow make it out of addiction on his own. The news hurt—not because I wasn't happy for him, but because his choice to seek help forced me to confront my own reflection. We were mirrors of each other, caught in the same web of mistakes, pain, and sadness.

That's the thing about close friendships in addiction: you push and pull each other to limits you wouldn't reach alone— sometimes for better, but too often for worse.

The next day, I spoke to his parents. To my surprise, they were angry. Their frustration was palpable, and they didn't hold back. I listened, then shared my thoughts about how best to approach the situation. Here's the truth: the way a family reacts can make or break their role in an addict's recovery.

Addicts don't start using with the goal of becoming addicted. It begins innocently enough, a temporary escape from a growing pain inside. But over time, the substance stops being a choice and becomes a crutch—a shield hiding the real struggle beneath. When that shield is stripped away, the emotions it masked come roaring back, raw and overwhelming.

As a parent, family member, or loved one, your job isn't to fix them. It's to support them in uncovering the why. What are they running from? Maybe it's a toxic job, a fractured relationship, or the absence of purpose or connection. You may not have the answers, but you can create a space where they feel safe peeling back those layers.

There was a time when my friendship with him had nothing to do with drugs. But when I think back, the memories that surface are mostly the ones we made while high. We'd grown to enjoy the high as much as we did each other, using it to enhance our bond. So when the drugs are gone, what happens to the friendship? Do you move on? Or is there a chance to meet again on higher ground, sober and stronger?

For friendships that existed before drugs, there's often a chance to rekindle what was lost. Just as addiction tested your bond, recovery can strengthen it. The power of friendship, when redirected toward growth and healing, can become something greater than either of you imagined. If you believe in your friend's potential and feel ready to be a coach or motivator, challenge yourself to reconnect. But do it with boundaries and clear intentions.

For friendships forged in addiction, the path is often different. These relationships are built on a fragile foundation of shared dysfunction. Keeping these people in your life is dangerous— because while you're trying to rise, they're still falling. And they'll pull you down with them.

Most of these so-called "friends" will mask their dependence on you as loyalty, using words like "friendship" and "trust." But your absence will reveal the truth. The higher you rise, the harder they'll fall. They'll resent you for leaving because you're no longer part of their coping mechanism.

Cutting ties with them is painful but necessary. Do not let them drag you back into a world you've fought to escape. Your recovery depends on surrounding yourself with people who lift you up, not weigh you down.

## What Lies in The Dark

Over time, addiction forges a strange relationship with what some might call the darkness. It starts in the quiet moments, those internal battles where you know the decision you're making is wrong but follow through anyway. Night after night, as you sit alone in a cloud of euphoria, something begins to attach itself to you.

It's like a spirit or energy lingering in the shadows of your life—

something no one wants to acknowledge, least of all you. But you feel it. You know it's there. And as time passes, you stop resisting its presence. You accept it as part of who you are.

This thing—this darkness—grows with you, feeds on you. Eventually, you become protective of it, nurturing it as if it's a part of your identity. And in a way, it is. After all, you've poured so much of yourself into this experience—your time, your body, your soul. Even if it's twisted and destructive, it came from you.

During my darkest years of using, I would often nod out on my couch or bed. I'd glance toward the darkest corner of the room and feel as though something was there. I'd convinced myself that something had attached to me, and over time, my mind gave it form.

What I saw was old, ancient even, like something pulled straight from a folktale or a nightmare. It didn't move, didn't speak. But its presence was heavy, and its intent was clear. It watched me, silently observing my every move, waiting for me to make the decision to use again that night.

To this day, I can't tell you if it was real or just my imagination. But in the end, it didn't matter. To me, it was the same. I knew it wasn't a friend or an ally, but I also knew it wasn't entirely separate from me. It was a manifestation of my own mind, born of my choices and my pain. And even though I feared it, I couldn't deny the connection we shared.

## Dealers

*Dear Dealer,*
*I saved a special place for you in hell,*
*Just a mile out and six feet deep from the spot you liked to sell.*
*I've spoken with the mothers of those no longer here,*
*They say there's nothing left in this world for them to fear.*
*You stripped away what they thought was their reason to live,*
*Yet through suffering and pain they've found much more to give.*
*But to you it's just another deal, another day,*

*Just know when your time is up, I'll pray that you pray.*
*For the path you walk is no different from mine —*
*The choices we make we pay for in time.*

Dealers come in all shapes, sizes, and walks of life. But no matter how different they seem, they all share one thing: they're in it for themselves. They don't care about you. Part of their hustle is making you feel like they do. They know the rush you're chasing and the relief every re-up brings. They want to keep you hooked—not just on the product, but on the idea that they're "looking out" for you. And if you try to pull away, the worst ones will reel you back in.

Over the course of my addiction, I had four dealers, each unique in their own way. Almost all of them were introduced to me by the same friend—my partner in crime. Thinking back, it's crazy how many connections he introduced me to. From there, though, the choices were all mine.

My first dealer turned out to be a kingpin of a large operation. He was always in stock, always ready. There were two spots you could meet him, and both were like something out of a movie. Cars lined up like a fast-food drive-thru. It was surreal. But during one of my hiatuses from using, his entire operation got dismantled. He was sent to prison, leaving behind a girlfriend and a daughter. In a way, I felt lucky I'd stopped using when I did—being tied to someone like him could've dragged me down with him.

When I got back into using, though, I ended up with a new dealer. This guy was something else—a real dirt bag, nicknamed

"Nasty," and he lived up to it. Most of the time, he was as dirty as his name suggested, but he had a silver tongue that could sell you anything. "Bro, if you throw me an extra $20 now, I'll hook you up next time," he'd say, swearing "on his daughter" every time. And every time, I'd oblige—because when you're an addict, maintaining that connection feels like life or death. More often than not, I got screwed.

One night, I met him around 1 AM. Looking back, it was one of the worst decisions I've ever made. Sitting in a sketchy parking lot, withdrawing and desperate, I waited two hours for him to show. When he finally arrived, he took my $120 and claimed he had to walk up the street to grab the pills. I waited another hour, but he never came back. He ghosted me, turning off his phone and leaving me stranded.

As if the humiliation wasn't enough, on my way out of the desolate streets, an undercover narcotics officer began tailing me. My heart was pounding; I had weed in the car to take the edge off the withdrawals, and I was sure I was about to get busted. Block after block, I waited for the lights to flash. For some reason, they never did. To this day, I don't know why. Maybe he had bigger fish to fry.

Karma caught up with Nasty about a month later. He was busted in that same parking lot, selling to three people. Their faces— along with his—ended up plastered all over the local paper. It should've been a wake-up call for me. One close call after another, the signs were everywhere, screaming that my time was coming. But I didn't listen.

My journey with other dealers continued for years. Some were more reliable, but the risks never changed. The stakes were always high, no matter who was selling. Sometimes I wonder where they are now, and if they ever regret what they've done. My gut tells me no. For them, it's survival. They know the risks—being ratted out, an overdose traced back to them—it's all part of the game.

But here's the truth: there are no friends in this. To think otherwise is not just foolish—it's dangerous. Dealers are players in a bigger system, and like addicts, they're hooked in their own way. Their survival comes at your expense. Recognizing that is the first step in breaking free.

## True Friends

*For those who stood by and tried from the start,*
*Keeping me guided through times in the dark,*
*You still hold me up, though my heart weighs more,*
*Than things first began and the pain you endured.*

*I strive to stay honest and committed to see,*
*Through what I've sought out to accomplish and be.*
*When life's greatest purpose is to live and be free,*
*I wonder why all this shit's happened to me.*

*The pain that we share it's not just to say,*
*That these paths we all choose there's no better way.*
*We try to find meaning in how things turn out,*

*To shine light on this life we know nothing about.*

*So as you observe and find solace in me,*
*Know I look back and pray you'll too be free—*
*Of struggle and pain it's the same we endure,*
*No different in time, just some can take more.*

Looking back, you'll see there were two kinds of friends: those who were truly there for you and those who never really were at all.

It's easy to get caught up in resentment, replaying the times people let you down. But the truth is, your problems are yours to carry. If you'd never messed up to begin with, you wouldn't be questioning who your real friends are. Addiction, though—it magnifies life's smaller struggles, turning them into tests most people aren't equipped to handle.

The hardest part is that addiction is seen as self-inflicted. People ask, "Why would they do this? Weren't they happy?" Because of this, only those closest to you—your family and inner circle—tend to feel invested enough to help. But even they have limits. Their support comes with an unspoken expectation: show progress. They're giving you their time, their love, their energy, and it's not infinite. Appreciate it for what it represents. Honor it by showing them you're trying. Without that, trust can and will erode.

Outside your inner circle is everyone else. They might have empathy for you, but they don't truly care. They don't have the time, and why should they? To them, you're an adult, capable of making your own decisions. They'll never grasp the complexity of your addiction—partly because it's difficult to understand, but mostly because it's not their problem. Until addiction touches someone they love, it remains an abstract issue.

Here's the key: you can't let their indifference derail you. Dwelling on their perspectives—imagining conversations where they judge you, pity you, or misunderstand you—feeds your ego and drags you down. Those thoughts are like a broken reel, playing out your worst fears. Instead of indulging them, redirect that energy into something purposeful.

Maybe your purpose will be proving them wrong—showing you're capable of making the right choices. Maybe it'll be in helping others, knowing one day it could even be them in need of guidance. Whatever it is, let it fuel you, not hold you back.

During your darkest times, people will act as the world does: some will help, some will walk away, and others will remain indifferent. This is an opportunity to practice forgiveness—not just for them, but for yourself. Their behavior isn't necessarily wrong; they're simply making the same choices you might if the roles were reversed.

We all deserve the chance to make decisions for ourselves. But the real value lies in learning and growing from the wrong ones. See yourself as a catalyst for transformation. Let your journey inspire others—not out of obligation, but because the future version of you would want it that way. And trust this: that person, the one you're becoming, is closer than you think.

## Protection

The relationship between an addict and a non-addict friend is fragile, a balancing act of understanding and boundaries. Some friends can handle the complexities of addiction better than others because they're able to delve into life's darker corners. Others will instinctively keep you at arm's length, not out of malice, but because addiction is a world they can't—or won't—understand. That might make your relationship feel strained, but try not to hold it against them. Everyone is learning as they go.

Addiction, in many ways, is a mirror for other struggles in life. Your journey may carry a stigma, but the lessons it holds are universal. Don't shy away from sharing those lessons. Some friends may respond dismissively, thinking, "This doesn't apply to me. I'm not a drug addict; I didn't make those mistakes." That's fine. Addiction is frightening, and that reaction may be their way of shielding themselves from uncomfortable truths.

Other friends will find ways to connect—not because they've faced drug addiction, but because they recognize the parallels. Addiction wears many faces: alcohol, gambling, food, sex, work. And the core of it—the longing, the pain, the need to escape—is something everyone has touched at some point.

Educating yourself and others about the nature of addiction is one of the most valuable ways to protect your loved ones. But protection works both ways. I remember, a few years into my addiction, getting calls from friends curious about pills. For those who were new to it or treating it like a novelty, I'd tell them to forget it. "There's no point," I'd say. It's like seeing a muddy puddle others have stepped in—you don't need to step in it too to know how much damage it causes.

On the other hand, friends often feel a responsibility to help. They may be the first to notice something is wrong. Their instinct to intervene is natural, but it's not without risk. The wrong approach can push an addict away, boxing them into isolation. To protect their own privacy and shield friends from the uglier truths of their addiction, addicts often create distance.

If you're in the role of the friend, remember this: there's no such thing as sounding the alarm too early or too loud. It may strain your relationship, but it's better than looking back with regret. Would you rather lose a friend to anger for a while, or lose them forever and wonder if you could have done more?

It's never too late to reconnect—whether during or after someone's recovery. But after their death? There's no coming back from that. The sacrifice of speaking up may cost you in the short term, but it's worth it if it means saving their life.

**KEY TAKEAWAYS**

FOR THE ADDICTS:

**Recognize True Friendship.** Real friends are the ones who stick by you during your darkest moments and care enough to raise red flags, even if it risks the relationship. Cherish these relationships and recognize their value.

**Take Accountability.** No one is responsible for your addiction but you. Stop blaming others and take ownership of your choices.

**Embrace Growth.** Addiction halts personal growth while life moves on without you. Acknowledge the missed milestones and use that realization as motivation to move forward.

**Reflect on Friendships.** Differentiate between friends who were there before your addiction and those you met during it.

**Let Go of Ego.** Avoid dwelling on judgment or misunderstanding from others. Use their perspectives as fuel for self-improvement instead of letting them drag you down.

**Find Purpose.** Whether it's proving doubters wrong or helping others, channel your energy into something meaningful to drive your recovery.

**Protect Others.** If friends reach out about experimenting with substances, guide them away from it. Your experience can prevent others from falling into the same trap.

FOR FAMILY & LOVED ONES:

**Understand the Role of Friendship.** Friends often notice the signs of addiction before family does. Appreciate their input and work collaboratively with them if they express concern.

**Support Without Judging.** Create a safe space for your loved one to share without fear of judgment or being cut off.

**Help Build a Support Network.** Encourage your loved one to cultivate relationships with positive influences. Share resources and ideas for finding healthy connections.

**Educate Yourself.** Addiction isn't just about substances; it's a coping mechanism for underlying pain. Learning about these dynamics can help you offer better support.

**Don't Fear Tough Conversations.** Raising concerns early, even if it risks short-term conflict, can save a life. Silence or avoidance can lead to regret.

**Set Boundaries With Friends.** Be cautious of friendships formed during addiction. Help your loved one understand that not everyone has their best interests at heart.

**Prioritize Your Well-being.** Supporting an addict can be emotionally taxing. Seek your own support through therapy or trusted confidants to ensure you're equipped to help.

**It's Never Too Late.** Whether during recovery or afterward, always leave the door open for re-connection. The opportunity for healing and rebuilding relationships is worth the effort.

# FAMILY

"It's not flesh and blood, but the heart that makes us family."
- Johann Schiller -

## Growth

**W**hen families face a challenge like addiction, it's natural to ask, "What did we do to deserve this?" It's an emotional, almost reflexive response— feeling victimized, comparing your family to others who seem untouched by such hardships. The initial focus is often on what the experience is taking away: the time, energy, and peace it seems to steal.

Only later, when the dust settles and things improve, do most families reflect and realize the deeper value of the experience. They see that while it kept them from certain things in life, it gave them something else in return. Their perspective shifts— from what the struggle did to them, to what it did for them.

Someone once told me, "Everything we endure in life is our

consciousness forcing us to grow, preparing us for something bigger." Bigger doesn't always mean more difficult, though. It might mean being ready to help others, to contribute to something greater than yourself. This person believed we all choose this life, with its unique challenges, because of a spiritual need to grow—not just for our own sake, but for the greater good of a collective existence.

It's a difficult belief to accept, especially for those suffering deeply, whether through disease, loss, or addiction. But with time, healing, and growth, we often find ways to relate.

One of my favorite thinkers, Jordan Peterson, offers a perspective that resonates deeply with me. As a clinical psychologist, his emotional intelligence spans countless subjects, and I highly recommend exploring his lectures or interviews. In one, Peterson is asked about the true meaning of life. He describes the example of a father's death and the oldest sibling stepping up to be the strongest person at the funeral—not just for their own growth, but for the family and others who can't.

This idea of stepping into strength during hardship reflects a profound truth: our growth comes not only from the choices we make, but from what life forces us to endure. The meaning of life isn't just found in our experiences, but in the meaning we choose to draw from them.

For families collectively experiencing addiction, there's something to gain for everyone. If they can remain connected and endure the process together, the struggle can forge a stronger sense of unity. The experience becomes preparation for something greater, a revelation that perhaps the family hadn't been challenged enough before. It's as if life is saying, "If you won't choose to grow, I'll force you to."

Now, you might argue, "Nothing can prepare me emotionally for losing a family member, no matter how much I've endured before." And you'd be right. The love you feel for your family doesn't diminish with time or experience. But if you face that loss while your own life is in order, you become a foundation for those around you. You set an example of resilience and belief— belief that life is a continuous cycle, meant to repeat in some ways but improve in others.

We either choose to grow with life's challenges, or life forces our hand. But when you shift your perspective, the experience becomes less about how it defines you, and more about how you define it. Everything we face stems from a choice—whether made directly or indirectly by ourselves or those around us.

Growth, then, isn't just a burden—it's an opportunity.

Rewriting Patterns

Years ago, I attended a large group awareness and self-improvement training. Looking back, it felt more like an interactive group therapy session—a deep dive into my past, guided by the idea that one or two formative experiences shaped both my strengths and weaknesses. The goal was to identify those limiting patterns, break them down, and replace them with something stronger. As new beliefs or outlooks were formed—often as simple verbal statements—they were reinforced by applying them to real-life experiences.

After two days of relentless self-exploration, a memory from my childhood finally surfaced. I was seven, holding my first report card. It had a bad grade—probably math. My dad, likely with good intentions, sat me down and began cracking my nose with his finger, warning me of all the bad things that would happen if I didn't do well in school. He listed them one by one: becoming a loser, getting sent to military school, and more.

From that moment, my outlook on life shifted. It became, "If you don't do X, Y will happen," a lens of fear and consequence instead of one of growth and opportunity. That belief shaped how I approached nearly everything.

But the past isn't meant to be harped on—especially when you're given a chance to change how it shapes you. Over the weeks and months that followed, I learned to recognize that limiting pattern. Slowly, I replaced it with a new perspective. Years later, I can confidently say my outlook—and the emotions tied to it—have transformed for the better.

We begin life as blank slates, our minds wide open, soaking in the world around us—colors, sounds, emotions. As children, we draw meaning from every experience, no matter how small. Think about how critical an impact that is: the strengths and weaknesses we carry as adults often stem from fleeting moments we barely remember. The meaning we assigned to those moments was shaped by the limited understanding of a child. It's like rolling the dice with no idea of the stakes.

Those early years shape everything—our relationships, our worldview, our sense of self. Most people aren't even aware of it, let alone given the chance to address it. For those fortunate enough to gain that awareness, it's a gift. It opens the door to unlearning false beliefs and replacing them with healthier, more productive patterns.

Thanks to books, social media, and countless other resources, we now have more tools than ever to rewire our habits. And it's never too late to start. Life will always be filled with the unexpected, but how we respond to those moments is what defines us.

One of my first emotional challenges was coming to terms with adulthood—real responsibilities, real consequences. I'd been addicted to a life without concern for the future, which is what drew me to opiates in the first place. What I didn't realize was how much of that discomfort came from my inability to say goodbye to childhood.

Instead of embracing the positives of adulthood, I fixated on the past. My mind stayed locked on the rear-view mirror, never looking ahead. I couldn't see the opportunities in front of me because I was too focused on what I thought I'd lost.

But here's the thing: childhood is only a part of who you are. While it shapes you, it doesn't define your future unless you let it. The key is to remain present and look ahead with optimism. Life is a constant process of becoming. No matter where you've been or what you've faced, there's always room to grow into someone stronger, wiser, and more fulfilled.

## Reflections on Roots

There are endless stories about why we fall into addiction. Most of them trace back to our emotions—anxiety, insecurity, depression—and the environments we were raised in. From our parents to the towns we lived in, from the friends we had to the fears we held, everything helped create the character we believed ourselves to be. But that character is often shaped by the opinions and perspectives of others, not by who we truly are.

We get stuck in that perception, convinced it's unchangeable. We tell ourselves that stepping onto a different path isn't possible, or worse, that it's not allowed. We worry about what others might think, forgetting that their judgments aren't reality.

When someone starts walking the path of addiction, reflection becomes inevitable—not just for them, but for their family too. Everyone asks, Where did we go wrong? But to pin it all on one misstep is shortsighted. There are too many variables, too many decisions, emotions, and circumstances intertwined.

Life is a series of lessons, and success depends on what we choose to learn from each one. We have more control than we realize—control over how we feel, how we respond, and ultimately, how we shape our lives. Everything we see, think, and experience can be re-framed with the right intention and emotional perspective.

## The Hidden Truths of a Loving Home

My brother and I grew up in a house filled with love and warmth. Our parents hugged us often, showed us care in every way imaginable, and worked hard to keep us safe and on the right path. My brother was someone I looked up to—his style, his confidence, his friends. Everything about him inspired me, and for all the right reasons.

On the surface, our home was a safe haven, a place anyone would envy. But like any home, it had its shadows—parts no one would see from the outside looking in.

My parents often fought, mostly about money. My father, for reasons I still don't fully understand, used my brother and me as a sounding board for the thoughts and emotions he couldn't contain. He'd share fears about finances and the looming threats he saw in the world. While we were provided for and never lacked what we needed, he made sure we knew the truth behind the curtain. It was as if he couldn't bear the weight of his worries alone, so he passed it on to us—right before we'd head off to school or into the world.

The fights at home weren't physical, but the shouting and cursing hit just as hard. They were like stones thrown into a still pond, sending ripples of stress and anger through our house.

The tension forced us to find ways to cope, to navigate the waves of emotion that seemed to crash in daily. My father was never physically abusive, but the threat of it hung in the air, always present. He likely thought it was a tool to keep us in line, but looking back, I wonder if it did more harm than good.

Despite it all, my father was more loving and caring than I could have ever asked for. I miss him every day—the good and the bad. But his influence, like every parent's, was undeniable.

As a parent, your energy and outlook on life have a profound effect on your children. You can't control everything that happens to them, but you can control their experiences with you. Those moments, those shared energies, shape your relationship and their perspective for years to come.

*A sketch of our family home, gifted to our mother the first Christmas after Dad's passing.*

## Version 2.0

For the most part, we're all improved versions of someone else—often our parents. Through their mistakes and our own, we strive to be better. Part of that effort is avoiding the same pitfalls because we understand the consequences—not just for ourselves, but for those around us. The other part lies in forging new paths, making choices they didn't, and pushing beyond their limitations.

This journey requires self-reflection, a willingness to challenge the status quo of who you are, and an understanding of your influence on others. Growth and forgiveness go hand in hand. Forgiving your parents for the choices they made—or didn't make—frees you from judgment and disappointment, allowing you to focus on your own path.

One day, you might find yourself judged by others. When that day comes, you'll want to know you did your best, that your mistakes were few, and that you learned from them. But what guides us along the way?

*The Ones Who Raise Us...*

Parents often plant the first seeds of imperfection in our minds. Not intentionally—they simply want better for us. Teaching us right from wrong requires putting us under the microscope. But sometimes, what they preach doesn't align with how they act. "Do as I say, not as I do" creates tension as we grow older and start seeing them as equals.

Some parents feel their job is done once we reach adulthood, as if they can stop being role models. But that job should never end. There's always someone to guide, always someone to influence.

*The Ones We Look Up To...*

While parents often take this role, it's not limited to them. Siblings, friends, teachers, and community leaders shape us too. We gravitate toward those whose experiences or emotions we relate to, seeing their decisions as a reflection of what we might do ourselves.

This influence extends far beyond our immediate families. The way we live, the energy we bring, and the choices we make ripple through every interaction. We should strive to live as though someone is always watching—not out of fear, but with a commitment to integrity. Working on our own negative emotions ensures they aren't passed on to others.

*The Decisions We Make...*

No one is perfect. We make the best decisions we can with the knowledge we have at the time. Sometimes we seek advice, but even then, no decision is definitively right or wrong. What defines it as such is the consequence—socially agreed upon or otherwise.

The freedom to make choices comes with the weight of social boundaries and expectations, and the right choice isn't always clear. Surrounding yourself with trusted friends and family can help you foresee outcomes and navigate the uncertainty.

*The Meaning We Take...*

The greatest impact on our lives isn't the decisions we make—it's the meaning we attach to them. This meaning shapes how we view our strengths, weaknesses, and identities. It molds the personas we create, which are intricate, intertwined, and entirely capable of change. Change begins with a conscious choice: to take new meaning from every experience, no matter how painful or challenging.

During that group experience in New York years ago, I heard stories that still resonate with me. One woman shared a memory from her childhood that shaped her life in ways she hadn't fully realized. As a young girl, she was leaving a store in the mall with her father and younger sister. Her father, in a rush, accidentally let the door close on her sister's hand. When her sister cried out in pain, the father turned back, yanked her away, and shouted, "What the hell is wrong with you?!" That single moment left a lasting impression. From then on, the little girl decided that men were mean and she didn't need anyone. Fast forward to the present: she had endured five divorces, all rooted in that childhood belief.

We're all guilty of attaching harmful meanings to our experiences—whether because it's what we want to see, or what others want us to see. Breaking that habit begins with clarity: separating yourself from negative emotions and seeing the truth for what it is.

This clarity creates the stepping stones for growth, allowing you to replace limiting beliefs with new, empowering ones. It's where the next version of you begins to take shape.

## Approval

What makes our parents' approval so much more important than anyone else? Like us, they've made good and bad choices, learned from mistakes, and grown over time—as parents, siblings, sons, and daughters. Yet, their opinions and assessments of our lives seem to carry more weight than any other.

I believe it comes down to this: our parents are the ones who first taught us right from wrong. They're the ones who showed us our imperfections, pointed out our flaws—not to harm us, but because they wanted better for us. So, when we succeed, we crave their approval. But when we fail, especially in something as serious as addiction, we hide the truth. Why? Because addiction offers nothing for them to approve of—only pain, disappointment, and shame. And, perhaps most significantly, we hide because we don't want the euphoric ride to end.

When we do share our struggles, parents or loved ones often play the "bad cop." Their reactions may be harsh or critical, but there's a reason we confided in them to begin with. Deep down, we recognize that sharing might be our best chance to get the help we so desperately need. In those moments, our need for approval shifts into something else entirely: the need for forgiveness. We don't just want approval for our choices anymore; we want to be told that our mistakes are okay—that we're human.

Is there a connection between approval and forgiveness? Absolutely. Both tap into the same fundamental desire: the need to feel accepted and free from guilt. Approval is affirmation—a confirmation that the choices we've made are valid in the eyes of someone we value. Forgiveness, on the other hand, releases us from judgment, guilt, or shame. At their core, both are external validations. They relieve an inner sense of doubt or fear by shifting the burden to another person's perspective. But here's the truth: neither approval nor forgiveness truly requires anyone else. True forgiveness comes from within. Yet, we often lose sight of this because it's our choices that created the pain we're trying to navigate. It's easier to seek validation from someone we perceive as having better judgment—a parent, a loved one, or even a higher power—than to confront our own reflection.

To forgive yourself is to acknowledge a higher power within you, one that already knows the truth in who you are. It's this inner wisdom that understands right from wrong, good from bad, light from dark. And it's through your darkest moments—the times when you've lived in the shadows—that you come to realize you've always been of the light.

Sometimes, we remain in the dark so long that we convince ourselves we don't deserve forgiveness. The weight of our mistakes feels too heavy, the judgment too harsh. To forgive ourselves feels wrong because we'd judge others just as harshly for the same acts. So, we look outside ourselves, seeking forgiveness from someone or something we deem more qualified.

But the sooner you realize that we all come from the same place, capable of the same mistakes and growth, the sooner you'll find the strength to change. We're here to learn from the greatest teacher there is: experience. It's through experience that our spirit guides us to remember what we truly are.

## Role of a Parent

Understanding someone's role in a difficult process, like addiction, depends heavily on the relationship between the two people involved. Personalities, experiences, and levels of trust all come into play. As a parent, discovering your child is struggling with addiction is one of the hardest challenges you'll ever face. Your instincts might tell you to take control, to do everything in your power to save them—but the truth is, you'll need to learn how to be an effective listener while letting them take the wheel.

This starts with a hard truth: you've never really had control. Somewhere along the way, something happened in your child's life that set off a chain of events you couldn't prevent, no matter how much you wanted to. Of course, there are situations where a lack of presence or responsibility as a parent contributes to poor choices—those realities can't be discounted. But I'm speaking to the parents who've dedicated their lives to guiding their children and still find themselves blindsided by this unthinkable situation.

First, give yourself and your family some grace. This is a new reality for everyone involved. Judging yourselves or comparing your family to others will only slow your progress. The truth is, every family has problems. Anyone who claims to have the "perfect family" is fooling themselves, and that's not something to aspire to anyway. Scars from life's challenges aren't weaknesses—they're what make you stronger and allow you to help others. Even though you may feel like a victim right now, one day you'll be in a position to use this experience to educate and support someone else.

## Trust and Letting Go

The relationship I had with my parents was built on trust, though they were always on top of me about the important things in life. The hardest part for them was that addiction was unfamiliar— something they weren't educated about. They didn't know the signs to look for until I told them myself. What I'm grateful for is that they let me own my process. And that's how it should be for most families.

If someone else is always there to bail you out, there's no accountability for your actions. Trust is crucial in any relationship, but it's not without risk. For example, we trust our partners to be faithful even though they could betray us. Just because betrayal is possible doesn't mean we have the right to be constantly suspicious. The same applies here: you don't want to drive your child away by micromanaging their every move, but you do need to establish clear boundaries.

Communicate those boundaries, and make the consequences known. I remember a friend's parents who had very clear lines:

if you crossed them, there were no exceptions. That balance of trust and accountability creates an environment where the addict feels supported but understands that trust can be lost.

## Shared Moments

One thing I've come to realize is the importance of shared activities with family that are free of substances. These moments can serve as anchors—simple experiences that are good enough on their own. For me, it was playing pool with my dad. He taught me how to play when I was five, and something about the game always resonated with me.

Pool required focus, which helped me escape negative thoughts and let go of bottled-up emotions. Playing together became a ritual, a safe space where we could be ourselves, shielded from the stress and drama of the outside world. Conversation happened naturally during those moments, but it wasn't about judgment. It was about sharing experiences and finding commonalities in our respective journeys.

Sometimes, all it takes is knowing that someone understands—especially when that someone is your family.

## Communication

During the first year of my recovery, as I worked to rebuild my life, it often felt like no one trusted or believed my progress was real. It left me feeling isolated, as though I was on a path no one truly supported. If I succeeded, they wouldn't believe it would last. If I failed, I'd only confirm their fears. It's tough, but the best thing you can do is keep focusing on yourself. Show your progress through consistent action, from your physical appearance to the way you communicate.

If you look at the timeline of an addict's impact on their family, the first thing to break is trust. When an addict isn't ready to stop, dishonesty often follows. Together, these fractures cause communication to stagnate, sometimes for years.

In my family, I'd say my brother processed my addiction the hardest. He assumed the worst-case scenario would unfold, while I believed I'd be fine. That difference in outlook made our relationship challenging. From my perspective, every interaction seemed charged with suspicion—even if he wasn't suspicious, I'd feel he was, especially if I was using. It became a cycle of perceptions and assumptions layered on top of a foundation that desperately needed rebuilding.

After my dad passed, everything came to a head. My brother and I finally opened up to each other about how we truly felt. It wasn't easy, but we knew something had to change. We considered therapy or mediation but ultimately decided to tackle it ourselves.

My brother introduced a communication method by Dr. Jordan Peterson that changed everything. The idea was simple but incredibly effective: during each session, one person speaks while the other listens—without interruption, retort, or debate. After listening, the only response is to repeat back what was said to ensure clarity.

The process had three key benefits:
    It stopped the natural tendency to oppose or argue.
    It forced us to truly listen.
    It ensured we fully understood each other.

Once the speaker confirmed that their message had been understood, we could move on to the next point. It was challenging, sometimes comical, but incredibly productive. Unloading frustrations without argument allowed us to peel back layers of anger, assumptions, and perceptions. We realized how often emotions create false beliefs. Experiences may make us feel a certain way, but feelings don't always reflect reality. That doesn't mean those feelings are invalid—they're real and deserve acknowledgment. But understanding why they exist is the key to moving forward.

Whether you're the addict or a family member, ask yourself: How strong is our communication? Reflect on the emotions you feel and consider the experiences that might have shaped them. Go as far back as childhood if you need to. This process helps you look into the "engine" that's been driving you all along and challenge how it's been built.

If you can encourage a family member to join you, you'll uncover truths and make progress you didn't think possible. For parents, communication is the foundation of your ability to help—it's critical. Without it, achieving any meaningful change is impossible.

For siblings, the stakes are just as high. Think about the future. One day, your parents, aunts, and uncles will be gone, and you'll be at the head of the family table. A strong relationship with your sibling not only affects your bond but also impacts everyone else. The work you put in now will set the tone for the years ahead.


## Interference


Growing up, my parents trusted my brother and me to make the right decisions. Their parenting style helped build the moral compass we have today. Trust was central to our relationship, and it worked—good decisions strengthened it. Of course, no approach is foolproof. My addiction wasn't a result of their trust but of other variables.

Even when my parents discovered my addiction, they maintained their approach during my recovery: they let me take responsibility for it. For better or worse, they didn't intervene as long as they saw progress. I wasn't at risk of losing my job—in fact, I consistently received above-average performance reviews. To them, that was a silver lining, a sign that I was holding things together.

But the question remains: when is the right time for a parent or family to intervene? How much patience should you demonstrate before taking action?

The truth is, there's no universal answer. Every person and situation is unique. Our worst decisions often stem from impatience, fear, or misplaced intentions, so perhaps it's time to rethink the word intervention altogether. Instead, aim to be involved in your loved one's recovery in ways that truly help.

Start by letting them know that relapse doesn't mean they'll be cut out of your life. Build a network of support around them that doesn't solely rely on you. And remember, even if you're the "coolest" parent in the world, no child wants you at their party.

To help you navigate this journey, here are a few guiding questions to reflect on. Checking in with yourself regularly can strengthen your relationship with your loved one and support their recovery.

1. How is your mental and physical well-being?

When life throws us new challenges—whether it's a job, parenthood, or caring for someone in recovery—we often think, "I need to get myself together to handle this." The better your mental and physical health, the better you'll be able to support your loved one.

Even if you feel like you're at your best, consider activities or practices that could enhance your well-being. Your health is critical—not just for you, but for the person you're supporting.

2. Would your loved one consider you a good listener?

We naturally approach conversations from the perspective of I or me, often relating what's shared to our own experiences. But true listening means focusing solely on the other person— without inserting your own story or judgment.

Ask yourself: How well do I listen? Can you give your loved one space to express their emotions fully, without interruption or advice? Becoming a trusted listener can improve your relationship and give them the outlet they need.

3. Are your actions driven by fear?

Fear is a common motivator, but it can be counterproductive. If your every action stems from fear, your loved one may perceive it as controlling or judgmental—and they'll likely push you away.

Consider whether your concerns are projections of how you would feel in their situation. To address your own fears and emotions, seek support for yourself—whether through therapy or trusted confidants. This will allow you to approach your loved one from a place of calm and clarity.

4. What is your level of trust?

Trust is essential but fragile. If trust has been broken, it's under-standable to feel guarded. However, a relationship without any trust is like a map without landmarks—impossible to navigate.

Establish a baseline level of trust, even if it's small. Let your loved one know that trust exists but can be strengthened or lost based on actions. This balance creates accountability while leaving room for connection.

5. Have you contributed to their support network?

Helping your loved one find resources—like therapists, support groups, or helpful articles—can make a difference. Approach this as planting seeds rather than forcing immediate change.

Share resources passively, without pressure or expectations. Let them know you're there to help but won't overwhelm them. This effort not only supports their recovery but also reassures you that you've contributed meaningfully.

6. How often are you having conversations together?

Regular conversations create a safe space for thoughts and emotions to surface. Whether you adopt the Jordan Peterson method or your own approach, the key is to communicate consistently.

These discussions prevent conflict and provide an opportunity to address underlying emotions, perceptions, or frustrations before they escalate.

By reflecting on these questions and adjusting your approach as needed, you can create a healthier, more supportive environment for your loved one's recovery. Remember, the goal isn't to control their journey—it's to walk alongside them, offering support when they need it most.

## A Letter To You

Dear Dad,

It's been two years since you left us, and it still feels like someone turned off the sun. The nights are darker, the winters colder, and the holidays less joyful than they used to be. When you passed, I thought life might somehow get easier, believing you'd be looking down on us, guiding us. But now I see that the easiest path isn't always the best one. It's the challenges, even the painful ones, that help us grow into something stronger.

I think about the good in me, and I know it comes from you. But I still feel like there's so much of you I need to live up to. Like you, I know I'm here to lead, to help others, and that's what I'll keep striving for every day.

I didn't do a good enough job of recognizing and appreciating what I had when you were here. I'm trying to do better now, but it's hard when the person I most wanted to make proud is no longer here to see it. The truth is, I took you—and the time we had together—for granted. Only now can I feel the size of the void you left behind.

You spent your life wanting the best for us, but the reality is, we never needed more than what you gave. You were everything to us.

Brandon

58

## A Winter Moment

I understand that not everyone believes in intuition or the unseen forces that weave through our lives. And sure, I get it—there are plenty of frauds out there. But this story? This one is different. This one is ours, and it will always be something special to our family.

Just a month after Dad passed, I scheduled a session with a well-regarded medium. My brother's friend had a profound experience with him, and something in me knew I had to try. The man was booked solid for six months, but that was fine— we needed time anyway. When our session finally arrived, we met with him virtually (pandemic times). He was everything we expected—sharp, intuitive, eerily accurate.

But near the end, he turned to my mom with something un-expected. He told her that at some point, she would see a butterfly—not just any butterfly, not just a passing glimpse— but a moment so unmistakable, she would know it was a message. He didn't say when, only that when it happened, she would understand. Mom nodded, took it with a grain of salt, and life carried on.

The next winter arrived—February, a year after Dad had passed. It was a Sunday, and the air carried that same heavy stillness as the day he left us. Gray skies. Cold silence. Something in the atmosphere felt... familiar.

I had just gotten home from the gym when I opened the door to find my mother sobbing. She had gone downstairs to do laundry in our basement. It was an old cellar, cold and lifeless, a place where nothing should be moving, much less something alive. But as she folded clothes, she looked down and froze.

There, on the ground in front of her, was a butterfly.

Not some delicate remnant of summer, not some lost winged traveler—an adult butterfly, vibrant, whole, and impossibly out of place in the dead of winter.

We placed it gently in a Tupperware with water and fruit, leaving it safe in the basement. The next morning, we returned to check on it—only to find it gone. No trace. No signs. We searched everywhere. It was as if it had never been there at all.

Months later, as winter melted into spring, we sold our home. The last day of our move arrived, cars packed, keys ready to be turned over. Mom insisted on one final walk through, a last farewell to the place that had held so much of our life.

And as she walked through the empty basement one last time—there it was.

The butterfly.

As if it had been waiting. As if it refused to be forgotten.

Mom carefully placed it in one of Dad's old cigar boxes, where it rests to this day. A whisper of something more, a reminder that love—true love—never really leaves.

**KEY TAKEAWAYS**

FOR THE ADDICTS:

**Recognize the Role of Your Family.** Understand that your family is navigating this journey with you. Their efforts often come from love and a desire to help.

**Appreciate Their Growth Too.** Addiction impacts the entire family, forcing everyone to grow. Acknowledge their progress and sacrifices as they support your recovery.

**Rebuild Trust Gradually.** Trust is fragile but essential. Be consistent in your actions and communication to rebuild it over time.

**Embrace Accountability.**  Own your process and decisions. Dependence on others to "fix" things will only hinder long-term progress.

**Shift Focus to the Present and Future.** Stop looking back at what you or your family could have done differently. Focus on what you can all do now to move forward.

**Communicate Openly.** Share your emotions and struggles with your family.  Honest communication helps strengthen bonds and ensures everyone is on the same page.

**Forgive and Be Forgiven.** Let go of past grievances with your family. True healing begins with mutual forgiveness.

**Explore Shared Experiences.** Engage in substance-free activities with your family to create new, positive memories that reinforce your connection.

**Acknowledge Their Pain.** Recognize the impact your addiction has had on your family.  Empathy is a powerful step toward rebuilding relationships.

**Lead by Example.** Your growth and progress can inspire your family. Show them the person you're striving to become.

FOR FAMILY & LOVES ONES:

**Be a Good Listener.** Practice active listening without judgment or inserting your own experiences. Sometimes, your loved one just needs to feel heard.

**Avoid Acting Out of Fear.** Fear-driven actions can push your loved one away. Approach situations with calm and clarity, ensuring your concerns don't feel like control or judgment.

**Establish Trust and Boundaries.** Clearly communicate boundaries and consequences while fostering trust. A balance of accountability and support is key.

**Support Without Enabling.** Offer help that empowers your loved one to take responsibility, but avoid actions that enable their addiction.

**Provide Resources, Not Pressure.** Share helpful resources like therapists, support groups, or educational materials without overwhelming or pressuring them.

**Foster Unity Through Shared Activities.** Engage in meaningful, substance-free activities together to strengthen your relationship and provide positive experiences.

**Focus on Growth, Not Perfection.** Celebrate small victories and progress rather than expecting immediate, dramatic change.

**Encourage Independence.** Help your loved one build a support network that extends beyond family. Independence is crucial for sustainable recovery.

**Practice Forgiveness.** Let go of resentment or blame for past actions. Forgiveness is essential for healing relationships.

**Be Patient.** Recovery is a long, often non-linear journey. Be prepared for setbacks and continue to offer support where appropriate.

# THE CHASE

"I'm holding on to what I haven't got."
- Chester Bennington -

## Addiction to the Game

Once you become addicted, your entire life revolves around your connection to the drug. Every decision you make is guided by the next high—relieving withdrawals and maintaining a semblance of a normal schedule. Scraping together money every day while lying to everyone around you is exhausting, and there's nothing glamorous about it. What most addicts don't talk about, at least until they've recovered, is their addiction to the game. The game represents the playing field—the moves you make to satisfy your need. From making that first call to your dealer to driving home with product in hand, those moments in between come with their own kind of high. And in the back of your mind, it's all for the ultimate euphoric experience. It's hard to recognize while you're in it, but you end up falling in love with the process.

The calls or texts from your dealer bring a strange sense of relief and excitement. The drives, though filled with intensity, make you feel like you're part of the game—a piece of the street culture you never belonged to before. As someone who came from a family and a nice community, being part of something dark was an entirely new experience. You uncover a different side of yourself—an image or alter ego that you grow to like in some strange way, especially if you've never known true hardship. Many people are fans of hip-hop or rap music for similar reasons. Why? Because they can imagine themselves in that culture, envisioning what it feels like. The sound, the vibration, the lyrics—it's the closest thing to experiencing the emotion behind it.

The same applies to the streets and the process an addict goes through. They don't want to be their dealer or anyone else they encounter on those streets, but they live vicariously through their connection to that world. When you're the only one among your friends who has ventured down these paths, it brings a high of its own. You're walking roads they would never dare to tread—and for damn good reason, because there's nothing cool about it.

Addict or not, we all have a dark side. For some, it's a place they've been forced into for survival. For others, it's a space they only explore through thought or imagination. And then there are those who delve into that dark side through other means: sex, drugs, alcohol, greed. It's all part of the spectrum of experience we choose to navigate.

## Dance with a Dealer

Every addict has likely shared a strange connection with one of their dealers. In some twisted way, it feels like they're looking out for you. It's awful to think an emotional connection could form in such a context, but to the addict, the dealer provides relief—a lifeline, even as they enable the slow destruction of your health and well-being. Most dealers are complete scumbags who couldn't care less about you. Others, though, know how to fake concern, playing their role to keep you hooked and coming back for more.

My daily routine with my dealer started with waking up and counting down to the moment I'd contact him. "Yo, you good?" That was the standard text, just to check if he had supply. Most of the time, he'd say yes, but I never really knew the truth. Often, he was waiting for a re-up from his own plug—usually family members or people with legitimate prescriptions. Either way, I wouldn't get my chance to pick up until hours later, just as withdrawals began to creep in.

It's funny, in a dark way, how withdrawals make the next high so much better. When you've grown used to getting high, the best hits come after the worst lows. Relief feels euphoric when it follows pure misery. So I'd sit there, calling and texting, over and over. The silence was brutal. Then, finally, my phone would light up, and I'd know it was on.

That moment was electric, a mix of excitement and guilt. There was always this gnawing awareness of the risk—knowing nothing was ever guaranteed, not even your life.

We had our usual spots where I'd park and wait for him. The waiting was torture, sometimes lasting hours. He'd text every 15 minutes, claiming he was just a few minutes away. I'd sit there, imagining all the other addicts he was stringing along, everyone waiting in their own version of hell. Other times, he'd call to say we had to switch locations because cops were swarming the usual spot. Looking back on the hundreds of visits I made, it's insane that I never got arrested.

I remember asking him once if he ever worried about someone overdosing or giving him up to the cops. He'd just shrug it off, muttering, "Nah," or talking about how legit his supply was. To him it was survival, and those were the risks that came with the territory, just as there were for me. Survival for him because he had to make a living, and survival for me because I had to support my addiction. It was a daily dance though that took two of us, and in the end that was the choice I was willing to make.

A Day In The Life

10AM. Wake up and contemplate how much I used the night before.

*Ugh, another blow to my bank account. That's it, today is the day I stop. I'm so tired of this.*

Staring at the ceiling, I wrestle with the reality of my situation.

*Forget it. I might as well enjoy what little relief I have before the withdrawals kick in.*

2PM. I've accomplished nothing. My bank account stares back at me, dwindling, mocking me.

*Christ, how can I keep doing this? How many more times before I finally break? Stop it. Stop beating yourself up. You've come so far. One day, this will all be over. You'll have your life back. Things will change—they have to.*

5PM. I wander aimlessly around the house, thoughts spiraling.

*Maybe I'll go out with friends tonight. Anything to distract me. But these withdrawal sensations... sweating at the bar, feeling tired and lifeless. No way. Screw it, I'll just end up spending sixty bucks out there anyway. Getting high is better. Safer.*

I grab my keys and head for the ATM.

*God, I can't believe how much I'm spending on this shit. Shut up. Just do it. Quick, like ripping off a Band-Aid.*

6PM. Cash in hand, I make the call and drive to my dealer.

*This is insane. I'm risking so much every time I do this. What if tonight's the night? The night I get caught—fines, jail, losing my job, losing everything. Maybe that's what it'll take to finally end this.*

I pull up and park, keeping my head low.

*Good luck with that. Just sit and pray you don't run into trouble. Get in, get out—you've done this a hundred times before.*

The phone rings. Relief. He's on his way.

7:15PM. Another call. He's finally here. I make the exchange and leave, gripping the wheel tight as I drive out of town. Every glance at the rear-view mirror feels like a countdown to disaster.

*What's the plan if I get pulled over? What will I say? Don't think about it. Just go. You'll be home soon.*

I hit the highway. Home free. But the relief doesn't last. A weight settles on my chest, a gnawing voice in the back of my mind.

*Stop this. You're going to lose everything—your job, your family, your life.*

It's too much. I crank the radio, drowning out the thoughts.

8PM. I'm home. Walking up the stairs, the same question plays on repeat:

*Is tonight the night I overdose? You're fine. You've done this a hundred times.*

I set everything on the table, planning my night like it's a ritual. Two pills crushed, a crisp dollar bill rolled. The first line goes down, filling my senses with that familiar taste in the back of my throat. Warmth and security flood through me.

*Everything's going to be fine. Relax. This is perfect.*

8:30PM. The next set. Not as magical as the first, but still sweet.

Hours blur together. The nods begin.

11PM. I wake up. One pill left.

*Maybe I should save it for tomorrow? Nah. Do it now.*

2AM. Waking again, the TV's glow filling the room. Mouth dry, head pounding. I drink some water and drift back to sleep.

10AM. Shades still open, sunlight pierces through. Outside, the sounds of a world that isn't addicted. A world moving forward while I'm stuck.

*Christ, what am I doing? I'm scared. I have no one to turn to, and I refuse to reach out. No one will understand. My life will be over if I do. This has to end. I'll die if it doesn't.*

## Close Call

It's wild to think about the sheer number of trips I made to score pills, each one a minefield of risks. The situations I willingly walked into—lugging cash into high-risk neighborhoods, doing something illegal, and practically announcing I didn't belong there—seem insane now. The nerves, the withdrawal symptoms, the shady transactions—it was all a part of the process.

Every day started the same. I'd wait until my dealer finally woke up, somewhere around 5 PM. Then I'd sit around for another two hours waiting for his "come through" text. During that time, I'd concoct some cover story for where I was supposedly headed. It had to match how long I'd be gone, which was nearly impossible because nothing ever went as planned.

Once I got the green light, I'd head to the ATM, dreading the money I was about to burn. I'd finally force myself to withdraw the cash—like ripping off a band-aid—and at that point, there was no turning back. I'd make the drive deep into the sketchiest parts of Paterson, NJ, looking like a target and feeling like one too. The locals had a saying: "If you ain't from here, you either coppin' or a cop." Lucky for my dealer, I was always copping.

The drive was always nerve-wracking. I'd rehearse excuses in my head, just in case I got pulled over. Once I parked, it was a waiting game. Sitting on some rundown street, anxiety bubbling over, I'd keep an eye out for anyone—locals, undercover cops, whoever. Every second felt like a gamble. One time, I ended up on Godwin Avenue, the city's epicenter of drugs, violence, and murder. Before my addiction, I wouldn't have set foot in Paterson, let alone its most dangerous street. But when you're addicted, your survival depends on the next high. The risks become irrelevant.

After finally getting my hands on the pills, I'd drive away with my heart pounding, sweating bullets, constantly checking the rear-view. And still, my mind wasn't on escaping safely—it was on finding the fastest spot to use.

One day, everything almost fell apart. I'd just picked up and was heading out around sunset, already in bad shape from withdrawal. Each red light made the symptoms worse. My hands were trembling; my body was screaming for relief. I couldn't wait anymore. I needed to use.

So, I did something incredibly stupid—I pulled over on the side of the highway. Desperation doesn't make you smart, just reckless. I balanced everything on my lap: a magazine, four crushed lines of blue powder, and the last dollar bill in my wallet. Right as I started rolling the bill, I caught movement in the corner of my eye—a police cruiser coming up the hill.

My stomach dropped. He pulled up beside me, window down. I couldn't scramble; everything was right there on my lap. So, I went with Plan B: act cool. I grabbed my phone and fiddled with the radio, pretending to be deeply focused on "fixing" something. When I finally "noticed" him, I rolled down my window, trying not to let the panic show.

"You alright?" he asked.

"Yes-sir," I said, keeping my voice steady. "Sorry, my phone's Bluetooth isn't connecting, and I didn't want to mess with it while driving."

He glanced at me, then nodded. "Good man. Hurry up and get back on the road—this isn't a safe spot."

I nodded, thanked him, and waited for him to drive off. The moment he was out of sight, I exhaled so hard it felt like my lungs collapsed. Inches from disaster, and somehow, I'd dodged it.

## Means to an End

Why am I doing this?
Why won't I stop?
What am I trying to find?
Where does this end?

The answers shift over time, just as everything that shapes you does.

*In the Beginning: Your Symptoms*

At first, you don't even realize there's a reason for your addiction. Awareness only dawns when the negative consequences start piling up. In the beginning, your reasons are often physical— pain, anxiety, stress. You use because you want to be numb, to escape emotions and struggles you don't feel equipped to handle.

Deep down, you know it's not the right choice. But you're young, and relief feels worth the cost. There's a defiance in you, a quiet rebellion against life, against others, maybe even against yourself. You convince yourself you deserve this fleeting euphoria.

To change course would take work—hard, uncomfortable work.

And who wants to struggle when numbness is so easy?

*Along the Way: Your Future*

Somewhere along the line, the question arises: How long can I keep doing this? You know you'll have to stop someday, but someday feels distant. Time is slippery—it stretches endlessly in your mind, then contracts in reality. Before you know it, the future has become the present, and you're still caught in the same loop.

By now, addiction has stolen far more than you ever thought it could. It's robbed you of opportunities, relationships, and the future you once dreamed about. The cycle persists because you've lost sight of where it all began and have no idea where it will end.

You haven't stopped because you haven't fully felt the weight of your losses. What you're chasing isn't so different from anyone else. It's the path you've chosen that's leading you further away.

*A Turning Point: The Reason*

Eventually, the weight becomes unbearable. The pain, the loss, the suffering—it all crashes down, forcing you to confront what you've been running from. The only way out is to go back, back to the beginning, to the point where it all started.

But now, the emotions and struggles you tried to escape have grown. They've festered in the darkness. To heal, you'll have to face them head-on and find what caused them in the first place. Even when you discover the root, undoing the damage and building new habits will take time—so much time.

The turning point comes when love for yourself intersects with belief in your purpose. Survival is innate, but thriving requires something more. When you align with something greater than yourself—an unseen future, a reason to hope—you start to create a new path forward.

Because as individuals, we are gifted with the will to survive. But when we connect to something larger, we gain the power to create.

## A Prayer

Work ended on a Friday, and I headed home to the three-bedroom apartment I shared with two friends. We had plans to go out, but a text came through—one of them wasn't feeling well. The other had plans with family. To a normal person, this might have been disappointing news. To an addict, I couldn't have been more ecstatic. A night alone meant uninterrupted time to get high, free from judgment or interference. It's sad but true: as addiction deepens, social activities lose their appeal. Being around others feels like a waste of a good high. They're too aware of what a "high you" looks like. And once your tolerance rises, you crave the solitude to fully absorb the experience. It's like needing silence to appreciate a movie.

With this unexpected freedom, I changed course and headed to my dealer. As usual, it was early evening—dealers don't like to work until nightfall. Even though he replied to my texts, confirming he was good, I knew I'd have to wait. Two hours later, sitting on a sketchy backstreet, I finally got my five 30-milligram hydrocodone pills and headed home.

Looking back, sometimes it felt like the journey itself was part of the high. The anticipation. The temptation to use while driving home, pills in hand. If you were in withdrawals, there wasn't much choice—you'd use in the car. But tonight, I was fine. I could wait.

I stopped at the liquor store for a bottle of wine, my ever-present companion to opiates. Rarely did I use without a drink; it amplified the effect perfectly. When I got home, my sick roommate was lounging in the family room. I used the excuse of avoiding his germs to retreat to my room. Closing the door, I felt the first wave of calm wash over me. My sweating stopped. Funny how much of withdrawal is mental. The moment you know relief is near, symptoms fade like they were never real.

Reaching into my pocket, I did a quick count of the pills. My heart dropped. One, two, three, four... where's the fifth? Motherfucker! Frantic, I searched every pocket, retraced my steps to the parking garage, and flung open my car door. There it was—a bright blue dot on the black leather seat. Relief hit like a flood.

Back in my room, I set up for the night. With a high like this, planning was everything. You don't want to waste precious time scrolling for something to watch. Everything had to be perfect. This time, though, I decided to double down. Instead of my usual

60-milligram dose, I crushed up 120 milligrams—four pills. My dealer would be around tomorrow, and my bank account was fine. Why not?

As I lined up the massive blue streak of powder, a small voice whispered, Maybe this isn't the best idea. But another voice chimed in louder, The high will be worth it. Here we go.

Boom. The powder disappeared, and I leaned back on the couch, waiting for euphoria to take hold. But something felt wrong. Panic set in. My heart sank, then started racing like it wanted out of my chest. Sweat poured. My tongue tingled. I stumbled to the fridge, hoping cold water would calm me down. My roommate was right there on the couch, and I wanted to scream for help. But I couldn't. My mind raced: If you say something, you'll blow your cover. He might call 911, and that'll ruin everything. Shaking, I returned to my room, clutching the water like a lifeline. As I set it down, the realization hit: I might overdose.

I dropped to my knees at the edge of the bed. For the first time in years, I prayed.

"God, get me out of this mess. Please, I don't want to die. I'll never make this mistake again."

Tears ran down my face as I begged for forgiveness. Seconds stretched into minutes, and I kept my eyes closed, staring into the darkness. Slowly, my body calmed. The opiates finally took hold, but the high was ruined. I sat there, shaken but alive, unable to put words to what just happened. Fear and relief battled for control. One thing was clear: I had gone too far.

They say fear of God is the beginning of wisdom, and this was certainly a start.

**KEY TAKEAWAYS**

FOR THE ADDICTS:

**Recognize the cycle.** Understand that addiction isn't just about the drug—it's about the rituals, the anticipation, and the connection to a darker side of life. Acknowledge this pattern to start breaking free from it.

**Give yourself grace.** The thrill of "the chase" is normal in addiction, but recognizing its hold on you is a big step forward. Be patient with yourself as you untangle these habits.

**Stop romanticizing.** The connection to street culture or a rebellious alter ego may feel empowering, but it's an illusion. You're not defined by these moments—they don't own you.

**Be honest about the risks.** Every drive, every interaction, every dose is a gamble. Reflect on the risks you're taking—not just legal or physical but emotional and relational.

**Trust your moments of fear.** Those near-misses, when panic sets in, are signals. Listen to them. Let them remind you what's at stake and use them as a catalyst for change.

**Survival isn't enough.** Thriving means more than just staying alive. Imagine a life where you don't need the game to feel alive, and work toward that vision.

FOR FAMILY & LOVED ONES:

**Understand the "game".** Addiction is more than physical dependence. It's tied to the rituals and emotions of scoring and using. Recognize that their behavior is tied to this complex pattern.

**Create trust, not shame.** Addicts are more likely to hide their struggles if they feel judged or cornered. Approach them with empathy, not confrontation.

**Be patient with progress.** Change won't happen overnight. Even if they recognize the problem, breaking free takes time and repeated effort.

**Look for quiet signs.** Behavioral shifts like isolation, increased secrecy, or frequent absences can signal deeper issues. Observe without accusing.

**Be their safe place.** Offer a space where they can share openly without fear of rejection or anger. Your support can be their lifeline.

**Separate the person from the addiction.** Remember, the addiction is not who they are. Empathize with their pain while holding them accountable for their actions.

**Don't try to fix it alone.** Their journey belongs to them. Support them by encouraging professional help or creating a bridge to resources, but don't shoulder the burden entirely.

# THE MIND

"The closer one comes to truth, the further one gets from mind."
- James Pierce -

## Illusion of Self

In the early years of addiction, you cling to the image of yourself that isn't an addict. It's a strange kind of denial— a refusal to let go of who you used to be. At the same time, it's a survival mechanism. You don't want to lose hope or forget your strengths, so you hold on.

The high itself fuels this illusion, keeping you in an overly optimistic state of mind where you convince yourself you're still okay. Even when the mirror reflects someone you barely recognize, the substance blinds you from the truth. Deep down, though, you know. There's an awareness buried beneath the surface: the person you've been holding onto is slipping further and further away. The pain of this realization is overwhelming, so you cover it up the only way you know how—with more use.

Over time, you drift further into the abyss, far from who you once were and even further from who you want to be. It's hard to accept, so you bargain with your own mind. You imagine a future where you've stopped using, because every addict has that belief: I'll stop soon. It's what lets you keep going, what helps you justify the next hit. But while you cling to a past that's already gone, you're also making no progress toward the future. Each use feels like a step closer to either rock bottom or a turning point—but the destination remains unclear.

At some point, there's a shift. A reckoning. You have to accept who you've become, because without acceptance, there's no change. Denial will keep you trapped, clinging to an outdated version of yourself while spiraling further into destruction.

No matter where you are in this process, remember: we all have illusions of ourselves. The key is to understand which illusions help you grow and which hold you back. Some of the most successful people in the world start with a vision of who they could be. They don't know when or how it will happen, but they walk toward that vision with unwavering conviction, putting in the effort to make it real.

It's not just about the first step. It's about the work you put in over time to bring that vision to life.

The point is, it's okay to hold onto your strengths—they'll always be a part of you. But it's equally important to accept what you've lost and what you've gained through the process. Instead of trying to become who you once were, focus on becoming the person you've yet to be.

## The High

Opiates interact with everyone's body and nervous system differently. For me, they brought the most incredible wave of comfort and euphoria I could ever imagine. My first experience was after injuring my lower back in college. It was like discovering a source of love and security I couldn't find anywhere else.

When my use turned recreational, I thrived in social settings. The high made me feel uplifted, open, and invincible—like I was on top of the world. Life felt perfectly aligned: I was young, carefree, and had every reason to celebrate. Using openly among friends didn't feel like a big deal. That phase lasted a year or two, until my tolerance began to build.

As my body adjusted to the drug, the experience changed. The same euphoria was still there, but it became less about socializing and more about the sensation itself. I started to prefer being alone, where I could quietly focus on the high without distraction. The euphoria I once celebrated with friends turned into a personal and private process. If I couldn't experience the high on my own terms, it felt like a waste.

The only exception was during withdrawals. Ironically, my worst moments of withdrawal produced the best highs. The contrast made the relief even more profound. I remember melting into the couch after a stressful day of work—it was pure bliss. But I also recall feeling an irrational anger at anyone who disrupted those moments. A dinner invitation or a phone call about something important felt like a violation of my personal space and, worse, a waste of money.

The high always came with a false sense of optimism. It tricked me into believing that everything in life—addiction, sobriety, work, relationships—was manageable or even perfect. I'd reach out to people to make plans or share big ideas, only to lose all interest once the euphoria wore off. Even now, I can recognize when someone's buzzed or high during a call or text. I understand where they're coming from, but I know better than to commit to plans with them. Reality always sets in after the high fades.

If you're close to an addict, watch for moments when they seem unusually upbeat or optimistic. While it may seem like a good sign, it's often the result of their high. They may feel their best, but they aren't at their best. These moments are risky because they come with lowered caution and heightened desperation to maintain that feeling. Be mindful of their patterns, especially during these times of perceived optimism. The false confidence they feel can lead to dangerous decisions—whether it's driving under the influence, overspending, or taking unnecessary risks. For the addict, it's all part of the game and process they've chosen to endure. Recognizing these patterns can help you offer support without enabling the behavior.

## Everything's Better Blue

My friends and I used to joke that everything in life was better high. In the beginning, there wasn't a single moment I didn't want to be high—everything felt better, inside and out. But as the years went by and my use increased, the symptoms started showing up.

First, there were the glassy, red eyes. If your eyes had color like mine, your pupils shrank to the size of a pin. Anyone who knew the signs—friends, strangers, even my own parents—could see the truth. Then came the withdrawals. Using stopped being about feeling good and became about survival. The joke about "everything being better on blues" turned into a grim reality: we couldn't function without them.

Life became a constant race against the clock, waiting for the high to wear off, dreading the onset of withdrawals. Withdrawal put me in survival mode but also filled me with a strange sense of excitement for the next use. It was wild how quickly my mind shifted between these extremes. One minute, I'd be in agony waiting for my dealer to respond. Then, just five minutes after getting the green light, my symptoms would start to fade—just from the thought of having relief in sight. For someone who's never used, imagine the feeling you get right before a long-anticipated vacation begins. That mix of excitement and freedom—like you're about to escape everything. That's what it felt like to drive home with pills in my pocket. Just having them was its own high, like holding a golden ticket to something exclusive.

There were times I tried to stop. Days, weeks, maybe even months would go by. But everywhere I looked, I saw reminders of those tiny blue pills. From the nightstand in my room to the center console of my car, they had touched every part of my life. The memories weren't just mental—they were physical. My body remembered what it felt like to use, the warmth and euphoria running from my head to my fingertips. That sensation was addictive in itself.

Over time, you start to notice something else: a barrier, like a thin film separating you from the real world. At first, it feels like protection, shielding you from anxiety, depression, and any emotions you don't want to face. But the longer it's there, the less you grow. If you never feel those emotions, you never learn how to cope, how to process, how to heal. When that veil finally wears thin and disappears, there's a whole world waiting on the other side. Beyond the initial shock of withdrawal and the long, drawn-out effects of recovery, you begin to experience life in new ways. Your awareness grows—of what you enjoy, of why you used, and of the role opiates played in your body. Opiates don't just dull pain; they release dopamine, the neurotransmitter responsible for feelings of pleasure and reward. Over time, heavy use tells your body it doesn't need to produce dopamine on its own. When the drugs are gone, so is the dopamine, leaving you in a state of physical and emotional depletion.

Awareness is the first step in reclaiming your life. Not just awareness of addiction, but awareness of your tendencies, your patterns, and the decisions that led you here. Addiction doesn't disappear, but it can be managed. With clarity and effort, you can take control of those tendencies and transform them into strengths.

Only then can you truly say everything is better—not because of a high, but because of the process you endured and the person you've become.

## Sacrifice

I try my best to take stock of everything I have in life, including my health. But it's not easy when we're constantly comparing ourselves to others. You push forward, creating goals and building a future with the confidence that you'll achieve them. With addiction, though, that drive begins to fade. Your physical and emotional reward systems become dependent on a drug, and nothing else in life can compare. The high becomes the pinnacle experience—everything else falls to the wayside. Over time, the cost and time dedicated to feeding your habit consume you.

Trust me, addiction isn't just about the moments of using. It's the endless cycle: using, withdrawing, and preparing to use again. This process dominates your life. You start sacrificing everything—your possessions, your relationships, even your health. And as you lose more and more, you start caring less about yourself and your surroundings. Without a foundation of strength, you lose sight of the future. Addiction traps you in the present. The present becomes about survival, and looking beyond it feels impossible. So you turn back to using, hoping to ignore everything you've lost.

Of all the things addiction took from me, the greatest loss was the path I might have otherwise taken. When I first started using,

I chose opiates to mask my anxiety. The relief they gave me was so profound that I didn't even realize I was losing touch with what I truly wanted in life. After college, I was the first among my friends to land a corporate job. At the time, I thought I was getting a head start. I told myself this was the path to success, to security. But within a year, I felt the cracks. The stress and lack of motivation were unbearable. Like many parents, mine prioritized career over happiness. It was the only way they knew to guarantee a stable future. I was terrified of letting them down, so instead of quitting, I chose to self-medicate. What's wild is that the opiates made me better at my job—or at least I thought they did. They stripped away my insecurities, boosted my confidence, and numbed my anxiety. I operated in the corporate world with no limitations, under the illusion that this career was a good fit for me.

Fifteen years later, I'm still in the same career, unsure of what else I could do. I've racked up financial debt, never met the girl of my dreams, and repeatedly chose the same path year after year. Looking back, I wonder: What would my life look like if I'd taken a different route? Maybe I'd be financially stable. Maybe I'd have a family. But would I be happy?

I'll never know.

In the end, I believe we're here to learn from our experiences. Whatever path we choose and whatever consequences we face, it's what we do with that knowledge that makes a difference— not just for ourselves but for others who might be walking the same road.

It's not about dwelling on what's lost but about finding purpose in the lessons we've learned. The sacrifices we've made can become the foundation for something better, something stronger. And that's what truly matters.

Rewired

Our brains control everything we say and do, relying on an intricate network of neurons connected to our central nervous system. Neurons, or brain cells, form pathways that shape how we function daily. These pathways evolve as we interact with our environment, and the patterns we repeat strengthen the networks associated with those actions. Over time, these repeated behaviors create "maps" in our brain—shortcuts that guide our decisions, reactions, and habits. Changing these pathways starts with a choice: the decision to engage in a new behavior consistently. That's the hurdle for many of us— consistency. New pathways require time and repetition to take hold, and sometimes the emotions tied to an experience can reinforce these changes.

Think back to the year before your addiction began. Can you recall any defining experiences or emotions? Childhood environments play a significant role, but it's often moments of success or failure—times when you felt rewarded or had to fight to survive—that leave a lasting impact. At the time, certain behaviors might not have been the best solution, but they worked. And because they worked, you returned to them, reinforcing those pathways in your brain. Now think about how you handle experiences today. How do those patterns tie back to your addiction? Years of drug use have rewired your pleasure and reward systems, making it difficult to experience life naturally. Whether physical or mental, your habits have been shaped by what you consistently choose to do—or avoid. It's daunting to reflect on how much your mind and body have changed, but the truth is, you can change them again.

The idea of rewiring the brain is both fascinating and empowering. Dopamine, a neurotransmitter central to our pleasure and reward systems, plays a significant role in this process. Ongoing substance use alters dopamine levels, reducing the brain's ability to produce it naturally. This disruption can leave you feeling unmotivated, disconnected, or numb. But here's the good news: your brain is incredibly powerful. With effort and consistency, it can create new pathways and restore balance. The frontal cortex, the part of the brain most associated with addiction, helps regulate decision-making, moral reasoning, and impulse control. It's a cornerstone of how we function in daily life, and like any part of the body, it requires care and maintenance. Awareness is the first step. Understanding your environment, emotions, and triggers allows you to manage how they influence your decisions. Tools like cognitive behavioral therapy (CBT), mindfulness, and meditation can support this process.

Meditation, in particular, has been trans-formative in my journey. It helps quiet the mind, offering clarity and calm a midst chaos. I'm grateful to my brother for introducing me to this practice—it's been a cornerstone of my recovery and growth. Rewiring your brain takes time and effort, but the potential for change is immense. With awareness and the right tools, you can not only undo the damage caused by addiction but also build a stronger, healthier foundation for the future.

## Meditation

Transcendental meditation is something I've adopted as part of a daily practice—or as often as I can. While I use different forms of meditation, my intent often varies depending on the practice. The most common goal is simply to unplug from the world and give my mind a break from the constant stream of thoughts. Transcendental meditation supports this with the use of a mantra—a word or phrase repeated to help detach from the flow of mental activity.

Another method I enjoy is inception-based meditation. In this practice, I count backward from ten and visualize myself sinking through layers, moving below the surface of reality into a new plane of existence. Each plane might represent a part of my body or mind I want to explore, or even a space where I hold conversations with someone living or passed. Ultimately, I aim to reach a place deep within where I tend to a garden—a symbolic representation of my well-being. I visualize myself repairing and nurturing the plants, fostering growth and balance.

My personal favorite method was taught to me by a spiritual healer. While it's less of a traditional meditation, it's a profound way to connect with what I perceive as my spiritual self or guides. I visualize these guides as a group of three to four individuals who respond to my yes-or-no questions with clarity and insight. Their answers often align with what unfolds in my life, making them a reliable source of guidance. In fact, they've supported me while working on this book, helping me overcome bouts of writer's block. This connection unlocks an immediate flow of creativity, as if thoughts and subjects are being handed to me as gifts.

Regardless of the technique, meditation has taught me the importance of being conscious of how I emotionally react to life's experiences. The more I can recognize and be aware of those moments, the more opportunities I have to break old patterns of behavior. From there, it's all about consistency. Whether in meditation or any other practice, our body and mind grow stronger in the actions we repeatedly choose.

## Identity

Your identity gives you a sense of belonging and purpose in life—a role to play, a place to fit, a lesson to learn. But as addiction takes hold, it begins to separate you from your old identity and creates a new one. Your story becomes centered around the addiction: how it shapes you, the lessons it forces you to learn, and the people you meet along the way. All the while, you convince yourself you'll stop—one day. But until then, you keep moving down the path of destruction, operating with a false sense of freedom to take risks because youth and time seem to be on your side. What you don't realize is that you can't become the person you want to be until the drug use stops. Most addicts imagine that day will bring them back to who they were before, but the truth is, life doesn't work that way. You have to start over—emotionally, financially, and mentally.

From my perspective, there are three stages of identity an addict will experience:

The first stage begins in the early years of use. You're still holding onto your old identity, unwilling to let go because doing so means accepting what you've become. The qualities and traits that once defined you are now undermined by addiction, and every step forward on this path leads you further into darkness.

The second stage comes as you dig deeper into addiction. By now, you've accumulated debts—emotional, financial, or otherwise—and you start to envision a future of sobriety. You're an addict with a dream of no longer being one. You cling to that dream through every high and low, imagining the life you could have if only you could stop. For many, this stage includes close calls, heartbreak, and losses that some never recover from. Those who do eventually find themselves looking back on these years with a mix of gratitude and longing. Gratitude for the lessons learned, but longing for the time they lost. After all, it was their youth—their prime—and they wonder what life could have been had they chosen differently.

The third stage is the transition away from addiction. By now, you no longer want to walk this path. Your identity as an addict shifts into one of insight and self-improvement. You seek anything that will lead you toward recovery. If you can remain on this path, it will mark the end of your identity as an addict and the beginning of a new life. While addiction may still be a part of your journey, you'll be moving toward sobriety. Eventually, you might even find yourself in a position to help others. At that point, everything you endured will feel like it had meaning—a unique set of circumstances bringing you closer to the divine and a higher purpose.

## An Honest Thought, Then...

I walk through the world with a sense of disgust, completely unimpressed and far from envious of most people's lives. Relationships, careers, images of happiness plastered for others to see—it all feels hollow to me. But deep down, I know my detachment is just a reflection of how I feel about myself. I don't think I deserve that kind of life anyway. My confidence is at an all-time low.

Here I am, a 30-year-old boy—not yet a man. Filled with anxiety, no money, no plan, and no real direction for the future. I've spent so much of my life being lazy that it's transformed me into someone I view as unworthy and unsuccessful. I can't maintain positive energy around others because that's who I've convinced myself I am. I don't have the strength to support the person I want to be. It feels easier to stay stuck.

I know I need to build better habits, to move toward something greater, but there's no reward waiting for me on the other side— at least, none that I can see. So I live in this endless loop, always needing to release myself from it but never finding a way out.

I stand here now, looking at myself and seeing someone pathetic and lazy. And the truth is, I've allowed myself to stay this way because I know I can get away with it. I've never really considered love—not where to find it, how to obtain it, or if I ever had it in the first place. Maybe it's all just an illusion, a bubble we create to trick ourselves into thinking life has meaning.

At the same time, I complain about it all while doing nothing to change. I haven't felt joy in so long that I've started to believe I don't deserve it. Maybe I never did. Perhaps this is it for me. Perhaps I'll soon fade away entirely.

## Suffering

"Suffering ceases to be suffering at the moment it finds meaning."
  - Viktor Frankl

I remember many times when I used out of anger or sadness, with nowhere else to turn. It felt like a deliberate fuck you to everyone around me.

"I'm going to dig myself deeper because I can, and because fuck all of you in the process. No one will enjoy themselves as much as I will tonight, or reach the place I'm about to go. If everyone else gets to live a life of happiness without addiction, then this high is all I have left. And if this is all I have, I'm going to enjoy it fully."

But that mindset didn't last long. I'd transition from that defiance into deeper self-loathing, using not just to mask the pain, but as a fuck you to myself.

"You don't deserve anything else in life, so just drown yourself. I'm sick of you, and I'm sick of this."

Those were some of the darkest times. It felt like I was willing to push the envelope further with every use. All caution went out the window. Breaking barriers—whether physical, emotional, or moral—became a twisted game. It was dangerous, reckless, and terrifying. If you're in this kind of mindset, I beg you to reach out for help. It's not worth making the one mistake you can't take back.

Somehow, I was always able to claw my way out. There were moments where I managed to take a hiatus from using—cold turkey, no safety net. But even those breaks felt like another way to punish myself.

"Here you go, pal. You did this to yourself, so now you can suffer the consequences. Feel every ounce of pain, sadness, and withdrawal so you don't forget. Enjoy your medicine."

Oddly enough, I found a twisted sense of pride in these breaks. Living without pills for days, weeks, even a month made me feel powerful. It didn't last long, but I convinced myself that my ability to relapse and recover made me unique—stronger, even. I wasn't concerned about the damage I was doing. I thought this cycle was helping me grow, but in reality, I was just feeding my demons.

To this day, I can't say whether my perspective was dangerously delusional or creative in its own way. Maybe both. What I do know is that if I had spent too much time being hard on myself, I wouldn't have survived. Instead of focusing on my failures, I painted short-term accomplishments as proof of strength. It was the only way I could keep going.

If you're suffering in your own way, you need to ask yourself: Do you believe you'll make it out of this? The answer to that question will shape everything else. If, deep down, you believe this isn't the end, then find the strength to silence the negative thoughts. Visualize what you've endured as building blocks for your path forward. Have faith that there's something greater at work.

## An Honest Thought, Now...

Life up to this point has been a struggle. When I look back on the choices I've made, I see a path carved out of anger and sadness. I searched for failure, almost as if I needed to prove my own loneliness right. It was me against the world—but in all the wrong ways. Instead of gratitude for what I had, I carried disdain for what I'd lost or lacked. I dared the universe to take more from me, refusing to believe in its power—or my own. It wasn't until I had been stripped of everything that I finally understood what I no longer desired.

There are still moments of anger, but I know I'm on the right path now. I pay attention to the signs, those subtle reminders to keep moving forward. Like most people, what holds me back is the fear of failure or the thought that I won't be great at what I pursue. But greatness isn't about the first attempt—it's about continuing to grow, step by step, no matter how long it takes.

When it gets hard, don't be afraid to ask for help. "The Lord is near to all who call on him in truth." Sometimes, you need to trust in a plan beyond your own.

If you're in trouble and need help, then ask—but ask with clear intent for what you truly need.

If you're stuck and need guidance, then ask—but only if the path you're on feels honest and true.

If you've lost hope and need light, then ask—but ask in reflection of the choices you've made.

No matter where you stand, you will succeed. The only thing that can stop you is yourself. It's been you all along—and it always will be.

**KEY TAKEAWAYS**

FOR THE ADDICTS:

**Self-Awareness is Critical.** Addiction often begins with denial, where you cling to an image of yourself that no longer matches reality. Recognizing this disconnect is the first step toward growth.

**The Illusion of Control.** The high fuels a false sense of optimism, tricking you into thinking everything is manageable while pulling you further from your true self.

**Break the Cycle of Self-Loathing.** Using substances as a punishment or "revenge" against yourself perpetuates a destructive cycle. Recognize this behavior and seek help.

**Recovery is a Journey.** You won't return to who you were before addiction, but you can build a stronger, better version of yourself through consistent effort and self-compassion.

**Embrace Change.** Rewiring your brain and creating new habits takes time and repetition, but it's possible. Use tools like mindfulness, meditation, and therapy to support this process.

**Accept Your Strengths and Losses.** Let go of the desire to return to the past. Focus on the lessons you've gained and the potential of the person you can become.

FOR FAMILY & LOVED ONES:

**Watch for Subtle Patterns.** Addicts may appear unusually upbeat or optimistic during a high, but this can be misleading. Pay attention to their behaviors and shifts in mood.

**Understand Their Struggles.** Addiction creates a cycle of using, withdrawing, and justifying behavior. Empathize with their pain without enabling their actions.

**Encourage Consistency.** Recovery takes patience and persistence. Support their small victories and encourage them to stay consistent in healthier habits.

**Guide Without Control.** You can't force change, but you can help by guiding them toward resources, like therapy or recovery programs, without trying to take over their journey.

**Focus on Long-Term Growth.** Recognize that the process of healing goes beyond stopping substance use. It involves rebuilding their sense of self, purpose, and relationships.

# CHANGE

"There is no beginning, there is no end, only change."
- Robert A. Monroe -

## Relapse

You've made the decision to stop, to change your life, and you're putting your best foot forward. You've mapped out a plan, scheduled the steps, and organized every detail. Your exercise routine is ready, your diet is set, and your expectations are sky-high. But here's the thing: no matter how perfect the plan is, expectations are often the weak link. When reality doesn't match what we imagined, that's when things fall apart.

We hold ourselves so tightly to these plans that when something goes wrong, we see it as failure—because we miscalculated. But maybe success isn't about executing a perfect plan. Maybe it's about how you respond to the unexpected. It's not about having a backup plan either; it's about being aware of failure and understanding that in those moments, you have a choice.

Relapse often starts with moments of physical or mental weakness. Physical challenges are easier to prepare for because they're tangible and immediate. You know what you're up against. But as you gain experience managing withdrawals, confidence grows—and with it, a dangerous willingness to repeat the cycle. What we often underestimate is the mental battle. It's less obvious, more drawn out, and far more complex. The truth is, the same mental challenges that led you to use in the first place will still be there when you're trying to stay clean—and they often feel even bigger now.

I remember my first relapse vividly. My only goal was to survive the withdrawals. I didn't look beyond that. Once the physical symptoms passed, I thought I'd take life head-on and figure it out as I went. But I wasn't prepared. At the first sign of adversity, I realized that the reward of staying clean didn't compare to the high. There was no alternative, no safety net, no one to share my struggles with. In that moment—and many moments after—I chose to relapse.

## Digging Your Own Grave

With each relapse, the fall becomes harder, and the climb back steeper. You return to a world of uncertainty, left vulnerable to the feelings you've distanced yourself from for so long. Life rewards us for our new choices, but it never forgets to test our strength along the way.

After a night of using, I'd sit with regret, staring through an invisible film that separated my mind from clarity. The world was still there, but it felt far away. One of the worst yet fascinating things about relapse is how it stems from a single choice—to leap again. I used to think that one choice would be easy to control. I was wrong. If you're willing to take one pill, one hit, or one try, then you're willing to drop all the way back to ground zero.

The majority of addicts relapse because we convince ourselves we're in control. But the truth is, we've never had control. The sooner you accept that, the sooner you gain control over what feels uncontrollable.

When people hear "surrender," they often think it means quitting or giving up. But the surrender I'm talking about is letting go of the limiting beliefs you cling to—the ones that tell you, "I'm fine." Let me tell you something: you're not fine, and that's just fine! We are who we are in this world, and there's strength in that. The best part of this journey is the incredible skills we acquire along the way. So stop being so hard on yourself. No matter who you are or what role you play, you deserve acknowledgment.

One thing we all have the ability to do—but rarely practice—is living in the present. Whether you're in addiction or recovery, living in the moment is a daily tool you can use. The past can't change, and living there won't make up for what's lost. The future? It hasn't arrived yet. Focusing too much on what's ahead can derail your actions today.

Most of us, addicts or not, are experts at projecting our thoughts into the future:

"How am I going to make it another week?" You're not. What you're going to do is make it through this moment, and then the next, until today is over.

"Work is going to be so hard this week, I hate it!" Tomorrow hasn't come yet. For now, take it hour by hour and focus on reclaiming the calm of living in the present.

No matter the situation, be mindful of your thoughts. Catch them in the moment and shift your perspective.

After all, this is your story and your life to live.

## Withdrawals

Once you become aware of withdrawals, they become another chess piece on the board—a constant challenge to work around. For those who haven't experienced them, withdrawals can be terrifying, especially the first time. They often hit after an extended period of use, bringing a harsh and jarring contrast to the euphoria that came before. The separation between those two states is drastic and unforgettable.

I remember my first encounter with withdrawals vividly. It wasn't like being sick or catching a cold. It felt like my entire body was under siege. A wave of crawling discomfort hit me, spreading through my hands and entire body. Imagine having an itch under your skin that you can't scratch—now multiply that by a hundred. It felt like a tantrum was erupting in every nerve ending. At first, I didn't understand what was happening. I panicked, Googling my symptoms, and the harsh truth began to settle in. Desperate, I started texting friends. One of them mentioned Suboxone and offered help. Within an hour of taking it, I felt relief.

That moment brought clarity, but also a sobering realization: I now understood the price of using opiates. If I chose to continue, it had to be with minimal impact—something I told myself repeatedly but could never truly achieve. At that stage, I wasn't thinking about the bigger picture. I was just trying to survive.

One of the most exhausting aspects of withdrawals is how they dominate your daily life. You expend enormous energy battling symptoms and hiding the struggle. Whether others notice or not doesn't matter. The physical challenge alone consumes so much of your time and effort, just to maintain your baseline performance. Where you once operated with the capacity to grow and improve, you now fight just to stay where you are.

As this cycle repeats, it develops a life of its own. You become accustomed to running at full throttle, always chasing the next high while fending off the relentless pull of withdrawal. It's a game of diminishing returns—one that will leave you in debt for years to come.

The fight against withdrawals starts with taking care of your body. Nutrition is key. Focus on healthy meals, and consider options like juicing or smoothies to boost your intake of nutrients.

Reduce sugar and foods that cause inflammation. Keep in mind that your drug use may have masked underlying health issues, which you'll now have to face.

Supplements and vitamins can also make a big difference, particularly those that support energy levels and digestion. Enzymes, for example, help speed up metabolism and reduce symptoms of anxiety like heart palpitations and sweating.

Beyond diet, it's essential to build healthier practices into your daily life. Experiment with activities like meditation, yoga, cold water therapy, stretching, or running. Each small step adds up over time, and recovery isn't about finding a one-size-fits-all solution. It's about discovering what works best for you and committing to the process.

## Letting go of the lies

One of the quieter but most damaging aspects of addiction is lying. Lies build gradually, starting with your first use and compounding through every relapse. By the end, they become a thousand-pound gorilla, weighing down every corner of your life. Each web of deceit leads to another, and another, until it feels endless.

If you've ever been in the position of covering your tracks, you understand the suffocating pressure that comes with hiding an addiction. In the beginning, the lies might seem small, even harmless, but over time they grow into a complex web. It's not just about where you're going or what you're doing—it's about the trail of crumbs you leave behind. When the truth inevitably comes out, every one of those crumbs has to be accounted for.

I took some pretty ridiculous measures to cover my tracks. I'm not here to teach you how to do the same. Instead, I want to talk about what it takes to let go of those falsehoods. Carrying lies is exhausting, and the longer you do it, the heavier they become. If you're asking yourself, "How do I start? Do I have to confess everything to everyone?"—the answer is no. That's extreme, for both you and those around you. From my experience, trying to do a complete 180 overnight often leads to failure. The key is to take smaller steps.

The first truth you need to face is your addiction. If you haven't already, start by admitting it to someone you trust. Coming clean now, before someone else finds out, can set the tone for your recovery. Being caught in a lie will only put you on the back foot with friends and family. For me, the first person I told was my mother. That conversation didn't instantly fix everything—there were still trust issues—but it was a step in the right direction. Admitting the truth gave me control over my narrative. It was my ship to turn around, but knowing I had help available made the journey less daunting.

Taking that first step—whether it's telling one person, seeking professional help, or simply admitting the truth to yourself—creates momentum. It's about spreading awareness, not just to others but also within yourself. The more you open up, the more life has a way of responding positively.

So, suck it up. Even if it feels like it's causing a setback, being honest is always a step forward. Letting go of lies will lighten your load and make space for the life you're working toward.

## Support From Within

It's easy to think of support as something external—something or someone to hold us up until we're strong enough to stand on our own. Support can come from many places and last as long as you need it, but if you see it only as something tied to your past, you'll always find yourself looking in the rear-view mirror. Instead, think of support as a force that propels you forward, helping you progress step by step. Even setbacks can be part of this forward motion, nudging you closer to the next breakthrough.

Support is everywhere. Every day, there are hidden clues and gems all around us, waiting to be discovered. It's about opening your eyes to see them. Have you ever found a song that resonates so deeply with what you're going through that it feels like it was made for you? That song has always been there; you just weren't in a place to notice it until now. A positive state of mind is the key that unlocks these possibilities, allowing you to see and embrace what's already around you.

For years, I had an issue with constantly swallowing out of nervousness when talking to people. It felt like a buildup of pressure I couldn't release, and the more I tried to stop, the more self-conscious I became. One day, I re-framed it: "Every time you swallow, it's your body holding onto the past." From that moment, I used it as a reminder that it was just a reaction—nothing more. It wasn't me, and it wasn't my present reality. That shift in perspective gave me control over something that had once overwhelmed me.

So, how can you keep yourself open to the support that's already there?

Find your way to positive thought. It could be as simple as a cup of coffee, a short walk, or any small ritual that brings a moment of calm. A positive state of mind creates space for supportive ideas and insights to come in. Follow the signs. They're already there, waiting for you to notice them. The actions you've taken in the past often leave breadcrumbs that lead to the answers you're looking for. Write down your thoughts. Keep track of the ideas and insights that resonate with you. Repeat them daily to build a habit of positivity and self-awareness.

Support isn't just something you receive; it's something you cultivate within yourself. When you stay open to the possibilities, life has a way of guiding you toward what you need.

## The What IF's?

What if I never went down this path?
What if I didn't spend all that money?
What if I damaged my health permanently?

What if this will never end?
What if I'm set back for life?

You can speculate all you want, but it won't help you—or your sanity.

There's something a little twisted in all of us: we enjoy taking those trips down memory lane, revisiting what could have been. You imagine the heights you might have reached if only you hadn't made those mistakes, ignored your instincts, or acted against the signs. In this alternate reality, everything shifts perfectly in your favor, and you're in a better place today.

But here's the truth: none of that is real. Speculation is just a shadow, an echo of a past that can't be changed. Your decisions—good and bad—are layered upon each other, each one shaping who you are now. Everything is connected, not compartmentalized between who you were, who you are, or who you'll be. You are the person who used for the first time, and that same person has carried you to this very day.

So, what is real?
Your pulse is real.
Your voice is real.
Your light is real.

The fact that you're still here, still standing, still capable of change—that's real. You have the opportunity to impact every person you come into contact with, starting today. Don't waste your energy on the what ifs of the past. Instead, focus on the what ifs of the future:

What if I turn things around?
What if I see someone for help?
What if I finish this book?
What if I can help others?
What if others need my help?

The world needs you in ways you can't yet imagine. All you have to do is step into it.

## Acknowledging the Voids

The weeks following physical withdrawals are some of the hardest. It's not just the physical discomfort—it's the emotional roller coaster that comes with it. As the haze of addiction fades, you begin to uncover voids in your mind, gaps that were once filled by using. It's overwhelming, and it's tempting to push those feelings aside or question why they're surfacing. But instead of asking why after the fact, try to sit with the feelings as they happen. In time, you'll start to notice the triggers that led you to use—and still can. Recognizing those moments is key. When they come, you'll need to consider other options, healthier ones, to respond in a way that moves you forward instead of pulling you back.

Keep a notebook or use the notes app on your phone to track what you're feeling throughout the day. Write down the emotions as they arise, and try to pinpoint their causes. The difficult thoughts and feelings won't disappear overnight, and that's okay. They've been building for years, from your earliest experiences to now, layer upon layer. Once you start peeling those layers back, you can identify the triggers at their roots and begin addressing them.

Addressing those triggers reduces the need for the drug, which likely served as a way to avoid emotions. Once the need to avoid those feelings is gone, your addiction loses its purpose.

The truth is, you already know there's no substitute for the real thing. That's part of why relapse feels so easy—because it offers an escape from facing those emotions head-on. But the only way through is to do the work. Explore the feelings behind your resurfaced emotions. Over time, the pieces will fall into place, and you'll start to see how far you've come.

Accept that this is a process. Good things don't happen overnight. But with patience and persistence, the voids you once feared will start to transform into something meaningful.

## Physical Change

If only I'd known how much physical change I was putting my body through all those years, I might have made different choices. The body adapts to daily exposure to chemicals—it has no choice. I can't help but wonder what issues may arise down the road, but I hold on to hope that there's still room for a full recovery with minimal long-term damage to my body and nervous system. It's remarkable how little regard most of us have for our health when we're chasing happiness, love, or instant gratification. The rewards of making the right choices rarely feel as compelling as the thrill of making the wrong ones. Looking back, I don't regret my bad decisions, but I do acknowledge the thrill that came with "breaking bad." Not because I enjoyed it, but because I could get away with it—at least back then. It's always a tug-of-war between living in the moment and making decisions with the future in mind.

Now, standing here in the future I once ignored, I find myself filled with curiosity—and confusion—about my body. I don't know if what I'm experiencing is just how I've always been, or if it's the result of years of abuse. There's been no doctor, no test, no clear answers. Just speculation and the determination to keep moving forward, to keep trying new things. The fact that I've held on without relapse is a miracle, but I know there's no shortcut back to the top.

Beyond the immediate and short-term challenges of withdrawals, there's no high left in conquering the climb out. Once you reach this point, you're forced to listen to your body's cries for help. For me, this has meant living with a constant state of discomfort—hypertension, daily episodes of hot flashes, a racing heart, and frequent "fight or flight" emotions, even in the calmest environments. Mentally, the toll might be even worse because the physical symptoms amplify the struggle. Many people in recovery turn to physical activity as an outlet. It's effective for releasing chemicals from the body and triggering endorphins, which can improve your mindset. This approach has its value and should remain a part of the recovery toolkit. But in my experience, physical activity alone isn't the long-term solution.

True recovery requires more than sweat and endorphins. It demands a deeper connection to a state of inner calm—something that acts as a control center for everything else. I've only begun to scratch the surface, but I've found potential outlets for this development: improving my diet, practicing meditation, journaling, exploring acupuncture, and trying cold water therapy.

Recovery is a journey of discovery, not just for your mind but for your body. It's about finding what works for you and learning to listen to the whispers your body gives you every day.

## Don't forget, you're an addict!

I've always wondered: do our addictive tendencies exist before addiction? If so, to what extent? Were they as strong or noticeable as they are now?

I believe they've always been there, lurking beneath the surface—maybe not as obvious, but always present. We've all experienced the thrill of reward throughout our lives. But an addict's mind takes that thrill and amplifies it, weaving it into a complex web of reasoning we may never fully understand. The goal isn't to eliminate these tendencies but to grow in awareness—awareness of the vulnerabilities that lie in wait, ready to trip us up. It's not addiction itself we should fear, but the life experiences that could lead us back to it. A friend once told me this, and it stuck with me. I started imagining the events that might tempt me to relapse and, more importantly, how I could avoid them. Over time, I realized avoidance isn't the answer. Life will throw challenges at us, ready or not. The real work lies in preparing ourselves to face them.

What are some of the addictive tendencies you're aware of? Can you imagine the challenges life might bring and how you'll respond?

For me, instant gratification is a constant battle. For as long as I can remember, I've lived life chasing the next big thing, the next source of happiness. Once I find it, I consume it completely, draining every ounce of joy before moving on to the next high. I often blame this on the world we live in— filled with temptations and desires, with promises of "more" that we'll likely never achieve. This tendency can be managed, though, with moderation. It's not easy, but it's a skill worth practicing—preparing for the more important choices life will demand of us. Our routines shape the emotions we feel. Right now, those emotions are tied to the old routines we've held onto. Starting a new routine introduces new emotions, essentially reprogramming how we make decisions.

That said, there's a fine line between moderation and stifling ambition. Sometimes, obsession is exactly what leads us to greatness. The key is balance. Recognize that even the most exciting things in life can grow stale. This isn't to discourage anyone from pursuing their dreams but to acknowledge the simple truth: nothing in life lasts forever.

If you've found a new path or direction, embrace it. Take it one step at a time, because tomorrow may open new doors. Stay aware of your surroundings, even as you explore, because that awareness can unlock outcomes you never imagined.

## Becoming A Master

People often ask me if I've mastered my addiction.

The answer is simple: no. I'll never be a master of anything—least of all my addictive tendencies. Sure, the addictive fibers that once controlled me are fewer and farther between, but even now, I can't imagine a time when I'll fully "master" it. The real master isn't addiction—it's life itself. Every day, I acknowledge its power, bow my head in respect, and say, "Not today." Today, life will not break my spirit. Today, it will not rob me of who I've become. Today will not be the first step back to rock bottom.

We're all here to endure, to learn, and to grow. No matter the task or the skill required, someone out there has faced worse than you—or if not worse, then something different. That's where our strength lies: in sharing and learning from one another's experiences. You've heard the stories of people who couldn't overcome their struggles until they found something "bigger than themselves." That concept rings true here. I don't believe any of us can face this lifelong challenge alone. At some point, we lean on others—for advice, for perspective, or simply to glimpse who we could become through their journey.

It's a ripple effect: the more you give, the more connection points you create. And with every connection, you gain strength in return. Recovery isn't about mastering addiction; it's about mastering the art of showing up, of enduring, and of growing stronger together.

## Values

The desire for more—it's what drives us, what keeps us moving forward. But what if you knew that what you have now is all you'd ever have? What if, no matter how hard you worked, nothing would change?

For most of us, this isn't our reality. We're fortunate to live in a world that encourages us to believe in the rewards of hard work, in the promise of success. But that same fortune comes with a downside: the possibility that we may never feel satisfied. How many of us can honestly say that we simply appreciate what we have, with no thought of wanting more? What would life feel like if desire were absent? Would it leave us feeling empty, aimless, or even questioning the source of our actions and what shapes them into habits?

We work for reward, and rightfully so. Effort deserves recognition. Without reward, there would be little to distinguish exceptional effort from mediocrity. But how often do we work purely for the sake of working? Like a carpenter who refinishes wood surfaces not for the finished product, but for the joy of the craft itself—how often do we embrace the process over the outcome?

The same goes for giving. We often give with the expectation of receiving in return. Whether we realize it or not, the intention behind giving is frequently tied to a desire to express something, or to reciprocate the expressions of others. This dynamic shapes most relationships—family, friendship, and love all boil down to a balance of giving and receiving. But how often do we give just to give? To buy a meal for someone in need without expecting gratitude or recognition? To offer help simply because it's needed?

And what about love? We love to be loved in return. What could be more fundamental to life than connection? Knowing that you're needed, whether for a lifetime or a fleeting moment, is the most profound gift we can experience. Yet, for many, it doesn't exist without that reciprocal connection. Together, we hold solutions to countless challenges, but when divided, those opportunities are lost to hatred. Still, even in the shadows of division, we find moments of attachment, flickers of hope that draw us back toward one another.

I'll admit that my life hasn't always reflected these virtues. But I believe, wholeheartedly, that it's never too late to change. Experiencing life this way isn't a matter of flipping a switch. It requires practice, intentional effort, and time—not just to better ourselves, but to inspire change through the example we set for others.

**KEY TAKEAWAYS**

FOR THE ADDICTS:

**Relapse is a process, not the end**. It's part of the journey, and how you respond to setbacks matters more than the fact that they happen.

**Live in the moment.** Focus on getting through one step, one moment, one day at a time rather than being overwhelmed by the future.

**Face the voids.** Addiction often masks deeper emotional gaps. Acknowledge and explore them to reduce their control over you.

**Be honest with yourself and others.** Letting go of lies lightens your burden and creates space for recovery and growth.

**Build support from within.** While external support is valuable, cultivate a positive mindset and be open to finding guidance in unexpected places.

**Address the physical toll.** Nutrition, self-care, and practices like yoga or meditation can help your body and mind recover.

**Moderation is key.** Instant gratification can be managed through balance and awareness of your routines and triggers.

**Growth is continuous.** True mastery isn't about defeating addiction—it's about enduring, learning, and improving every day.

FOR FAMILY & LOVED ONES:

**Understand relapse.** It's a natural part of recovery, not a sign of failure or weakness.

**Offer support without judgment.** Be a listening ear and a source of encouragement, rather than trying to control or fix the situation.

**Promote honesty.** Create an environment where your loved one feels safe being truthful about their struggles.

**Recognize their effort.** Recovery is hard work. Acknowledge the small victories and progress along the way.

**Educate yourself.** Learn about addiction and recovery to better understand what your loved one is going through.

**Avoid enabling behavior.** Set healthy boundaries that support their recovery without sacrificing your own well-being.

**Encourage self-discovery.** Help them explore healthy outlets and new routines that foster personal growth and emotional balance.

**Be patient.** Recovery takes time, and healing is not linear. Stay present and celebrate incremental progress.

# A WAY OUT

"The only way out is to climb."
- Cheryl Strayed -

## Balance

Finding a balance between what you have and what you don't can be a turning point in your recovery. Whatever resources you have—whether it's time, money, or relationships—addiction will consume them effortlessly if left unchecked. Each of us comes from a different background, some rich and some poor, but addiction doesn't discriminate. It chews through everything indiscriminately, leaving behind only what you're willing to fight to protect.

The truth is, we all place value on life and material things differently. For many addicts, life itself loses its value, and the opportunities it presents each day go unnoticed. This lack of value can lead to careless decisions, unnecessary risks, and, inevitably, the concept we all know too well: rock bottom.

But rock bottom isn't just a single moment or event—it's layered. Beneath the initial fall lies a story of gradual erosion. Long before addiction took hold, we were accustomed to a way of living where we saw potential in ourselves. We dreamed of who we could become. Over time, often without realizing it, that image of ourselves corroded. By the time we noticed, we'd already lost more than we could afford.

Here's the hard truth: it's only a matter of time before addiction strips away what remains. And if you choose to exit this cycle, there's only one way out—you have to do the work. There are no shortcuts. What you put into your recovery, you'll get back. No matter your circumstances, your future is in your hands.

## A Choice

I grew up in a small town in North Jersey, the kind of place where family and friends created a unique energy all their own. News traveled fast, often blending truth with gossip in a way that made escape nearly impossible. It was a town with a front-and-center spotlight on everyone, yet it still felt private and cozy. Even the best of people eventually seemed to hit their limit living there. One of those people was my pee wee football coach.

I was seven years old when I first met Coach. It was at my older brother's football awards ceremony, an event everyone in town called the "beefsteak dinner." Every team, from the youngest juniors to the oldest players, came together for the awards, but the real highlight was the meal: tender cuts of beef served over toasted bread. I remember sitting at a table with my parents when Coach approached and introduced himself. He told us he was starting our town's very first pee wee football team. Up until then, kids had to wait a bit longer to play, starting at the junior level. Coach was recruiting kids to fill the new team, and since I wanted to do everything my older brother did, I immediately said yes.

The next few years were both challenging and exciting. Our team was often an average of one to two years younger than the others in the area. The age gap meant significant size differences, and I was on the smaller end of the scale—much smaller. But what no one, including myself, realized was just how fast I was. Not only was I quick, but I wasn't afraid to hit or get hit. That combination made me the team's star running back and most valuable player. Over two seasons, I scored countless touchdowns, and even though we often lost, those moments on the field were unforgettable.

One game stands out above all others: the day we played Pequannock. Everyone knew facing them was a death sentence— they were the number one team in the state. But somehow, I managed to score three touchdowns, and we tied the unbeatable team. After my third touchdown, I ran off the field in sheer excitement. Coach picked me up in a massive hug, and in that moment, I felt pure happiness. It's a memory I'll carry with me forever.

Years later, after I had graduated high school, I learned that Coach's son had passed away from an accidental overdose. It was one of the first tragedies in our town tied to the opioid epidemic that was sweeping the country. I can't recall exactly how or why, but I reached out to Coach—not just to offer my condolences, but to tell him I was struggling with addiction too. That moment sparked a dialogue between us, and eventually, we spoke over the phone. Looking back, we were both still deeply in our pain. I was in the thick of my addiction, and he was navigating the unimaginable loss of his son.

One day, we decided to meet in person. We went to a New York Rangers game at Madison Square Garden and met for dinner beforehand. It was the first time I had seen him since I was a kid, and the hug he gave me felt almost the same. This time, though, the emotions were more complex—happy, but different. Over dinner, we talked about family, football, and the past, but also the harsh reality that had brought us back together. With tears in his eyes, Coach shared the depth of his loss and made me promise him one thing: that I would survive. That I would find my way out of this mess.

At the time, I didn't fully grasp how significant that moment was. It wasn't an immediate turning point, but it planted a seed that grew over the next few years. The choice to reconnect with him, to have that conversation, became a cornerstone of my recovery.

There's something powerful about the foundation of our childhood experiences, including the people who shaped us. Addiction changes us, and it's important to focus on the future, but sometimes, revisiting the past reminds us of what we still have. Coach has played a vital role in my life—not just once, but twice. I'm grateful for his presence during those critical moments.

If there's someone in your life you've thought about recon- necting with, don't hesitate. There's a unique energy and emotion in revisiting your past that can remind you of who you are. No matter the challenge or how much we've changed, our paths have always been leading us to where we are today. And sometimes, through our own recovery, we may find ourselves helping others navigate their way out as well.

## The Fence

I'm standing at the edge of something monumental, caught in a place where freedom feels just inches away. At the same time, I know how easy it would be to slip back to square one. It's like teetering on the edge of a fence, with a clear view of both sides—one filled with light and possibility, the other a pit of darkness I've climbed out of before. And because I'm right there, balanced on the line, I keep jumping back and forth.

I know what it's like to live in the dark, to have your only goal for years be climbing out of it. So many of my memories are tied to that darkness. And now, for the first time, I have the power to choose. I'm no longer physically addicted, but that's its own kind of danger. This position of choice is powerful yet precarious. Faith in my decisions—whether they're right or wrong—is the only thing that keeps me moving forward.

But some things in this journey aren't up for debate. There are parts of this process that simply can't be juggled. Finances are a glaring example. Addiction is a money pit that always leaves you scraping by, desperate just to survive. Then there's the physical and mental toll, which is even greater.

After coming clean about my addiction, my therapist once told me I was one of the most dangerous addicts he'd worked with. It wasn't a compliment, though my twisted mind almost took it as one. He said it because of my ability to keep bouncing back, taking hit after hit—physically, mentally, emotionally—only to dive back in again. At the time, I laughed. I was proud of how far I could push myself. But as I grow older, I see the reality: this train can't keep running forever. At some point, it'll break down. Thinking otherwise would be naive.

Where do you see yourself on this journey, whether you're the addict or a loved one? Wherever you think you are, it might not match reality. Not because your judgment is off, but because we all tend to misjudge the distance between where we stand and where we think we'll finish. We imagine a clear finish line, a moment when it all ends. But the truth is, it never ends. Recovery is a lifetime experience, a series of smaller finish lines you only recognize in hindsight.

A close friend of mine has a way of drawing addicts into her life—friends, family, strangers. She once told me it's not the addiction or the drugs we should fear, but where the addiction might take us next. When we're numb to the world, there's no concern for how deep we go. That's the real danger.

So wherever you are on this path, be honest about the darkness. Don't lose sight of the light, even when it feels far away. This journey will demand constant awareness, filled with pain, love, and moments of joy. Look for the signs along the way. Life has a way of placing markers for us, higher powers nudging us forward. The key is to stay open—just a little. That's all it takes to see the world of possibilities that's been waiting for you all along.

"Your way" out..

After hearing the wisdom of countless seasoned addicts, one truth stands out: there is no universal path to sobriety.

Don't confuse this with the idea that there's no way to fight addiction—there are plenty of treatment options and methods available. But no matter how many success stories you hear or approaches you try to emulate, no single solution will fit your journey perfectly. As I said in the introduction, the only person who can truly turn things around for the addict is the addict themselves. It all starts with a decision—a deeply personal one. And for family and friends, it's crucial to recognize that the addict owns that decision, not you.

One of the hardest parts of supporting an addict is finding the balance between caring and stepping back to let them manage their recovery. If they ask for your help, jump in and engage in the decision-making process. But if they insist on taking the reins, respect that choice. Just as it was their decision to take the first pill, it must be their decision to take the first step out of addiction. There will be moments of disagreement—it's inevitable. Emotions and old patterns of response will surface as the addict begins to unravel their relationship with addiction. But don't let that stop you from voicing your thoughts. If your loved one has truly made the decision to stop, they will eventually welcome your advice, even if they're not ready to hear it in the moment.

To illustrate the delicate dynamic of communication, let me share a text exchange I had with my brother not long after I moved to a new city and began a new lifestyle:

*Brother*: How's things, good? A little worried about your overall well-being.

*Me*: I don't understand why you drop the "I'm worried" comments. What are you worried about if I'm not? This place and the friends here are good for me.

*Brother*: You don't have to get it; it's just my natural concern. How do I know what's going on in your world?

*Me*: I get it, but saying you're worried doesn't put anything positive out there. It comes off as you having doubts, not optimism.

We spoke briefly after this, but neither of us fully budged on our perspectives. At the time, I was one month sober and navigating life without addiction. Everything wasn't perfect, but it wasn't bad either. I was learning to live without the constant weight of addiction on my mind. So, when my brother expressed his worry, it felt like he'd thrown a small stone into the pond of my mental tranquility. His words rippled through me, creating unnecessary disturbance.

In hindsight, I can see I overreacted. My response wasn't balanced—it was defensive, shaped by the fragile mental state I was in. From my brother's perspective, his comment was meant to express empathy, not suspicion. Could I have handled it better? Absolutely. And moving forward, I did. But to get there, I first had to achieve a more grounded state of mind, one less easily shaken by well-intended remarks.

Communication between addicts and their loved ones is going to be messy at first. There will be misunderstandings, missteps, and frustration. But over time, if both sides commit to the process, it can evolve into something stronger and healthier than ever before.

Building this bridge takes time, but the reward is worth the effort: a support system rooted in understanding, trust, and mutual respect. Together, you can navigate the ups and downs of recovery, growing stronger with each step forward.

## The Fight

For an addict, stopping isn't a one-time decision—it's a fight with many rounds. True progress begins with understanding why you started using in the first place. Without that inner work, attempts to change often result in a cycle of relapse. Change must come from the inside out; those who try to transform from the outside in often find themselves back where they started. At this point in my journey, I don't fully know where my happiness comes from. Is it my environment, my friends, my family, or the opiates I've relied on for so long? Maybe it's all of the above. I used drugs to turn up the volume on experiences I already enjoyed, convinced that without them, the moment would pass me by or wouldn't feel as special.

We all reflect on our lives through the lens of opportunities seized or lost. For many, it feels like there's more regret than triumph. But what if the results of our lives weren't tied to specific events or missed chances? Most people view their past as a series of things that happened to them. Others see those experiences as something they had a hand in shaping. It's not easy to notice while you're in the thick of your story, but being too wrapped up in your narrative can blind you to life's broader possibilities—and to your ability to choose differently.

For many addicts, the first steps toward sobriety often take the form of an aggressive, all-or-nothing 180-degree turnaround. These efforts are usually fueled by a traumatic event: the loss of a loved one, financial ruin, legal troubles, or an overwhelming sense of guilt. While stories of rapid and resolute transformation are inspiring, they're not the reality for everyone. And that's okay.

Take, for example, a friend who announces their intention to stop using and live the life they've always dreamed of. When asked if they plan to use again, they answer, "No, this is it for me. Never again." Hearing those words is uplifting—it's a sign that they've tapped into a desire for something greater and are trusting in the unknowns of a life without drugs. But no matter how genuine their intention, it's important to remind them to level-set their expectations. That doesn't mean assuming they'll relapse, but rather creating space for forgiveness if they do. Recovery is a deeply personal path. There is no "right" or "wrong" way—there is only their way.

I went to see a film recently about the rise and fall of one of my favorite bands, LCD Soundsystem. In an interview, their lead singer, James Murphy, was asked what he thought the group's biggest failure was. He explained that for most great musicians or bands, their defining moment comes at the intersection of their greatest potential and their greatest failure. For LCD Soundsystem, that moment was their decision to disband after a successful 10-year run. His response struck me as honest but incomplete. It made me question how we, as humans, define failure. Failure is inevitable; it's how we learn, grow, and evolve. Yet we often see it as a detour, a roadblock, or even the end of progress. Rarely do we recognize failure for what it truly is: a necessary part of the journey.

Life is constantly changing, and it's hard to know when—or if—we'll feel satisfied. But one thing is certain: we weren't meant to live by rigid standards of success or follow per-determined paths. Instead, we're meant to struggle and fight. It's through that fight, through the daily grind and inevitable suffering, that we come to those rare moments of clarity. And it's those moments that have the power to spark real change.

So, keep fighting. Keep struggling. Let the hard days shape you. And when those moments of clarity come, let them be the fuel for a new chapter in your story.

## Barriers

When people think about the difficulty of overcoming addiction, they often fixate on the physical aspects: detox, withdrawals, and cravings. What they fail to grasp is how long and drawn-out the mental battle truly is. For those of us who've been addicted for years, we're stuck in a pattern that's not just hard to stop but equally difficult to replace. Everywhere you look, you see life through the lens of an addicted mind. You might think you see pills sitting on your nightstand or instinctively check your pockets for hidden stashes. Even something as simple as plastic sandwich wrap can transport you back to the moments of picking up product from your dealer.

But beyond these daily mental triggers lies another layer: the barriers that prevent you from taking that first step toward freedom. Depending on your situation, cutting ties and walking away may not be as simple as it sounds.

Take one of my friends, for example. His network of dealers seemed endless, making it nearly impossible for him to escape. He eventually had to change his number and even relocate to stand a chance. My situation was less complicated, as I only dealt with two people. One was arrested, and the other I slowly distanced myself from. But "cutting ties" isn't an overnight process. It took months of starting and stopping, relapsing and retrying. Each time I tried to pull away, my dealer would encourage me to come back. "Nah, bro, you've got this. Ain't no problem," he'd say. He was full of shit, and we both knew it.

And it's not just the dealers. Fellow addicts can pull you back in just as quickly. They might text, asking if you want to split a deal or use together to soften the loneliness of it all. Some of my most enjoyable—yet toxic—times using were with friends because it distracted me from the depressing reality of addiction. Severing those friendships was one of the hardest steps. I had to accept that while we might reconnect one day, it might never happen. Two of my closest friends didn't even show up to my dad's funeral. At first, I was angry. But over time, I realized they might still be trapped in their own battles, unable to face a situation that could trigger them.

For me, the hardest and most multi-layered barrier to overcome was how I handled everyday life without the numbing comfort of drugs. For years, I navigated life under a protective film of warmth and euphoria that took the edge off every difficult moment. No matter how hard the day was, I always had the evening's escape to look forward to. But years of use had wreaked havoc on my body and nervous system, leaving me physically broken in ways I couldn't ignore. Socializing and communicating felt impossible. I was always sweating and constantly uncomfortable—like walking around with a rock in my shoe. I kept hoping the symptoms would fade on their own, but they didn't. That ongoing discomfort became my breaking point and the reason I relapsed so many times.

Eventually, I realized I couldn't just "wait it out." I had to actively heal my body. My turning point came when I found a doctor who understood the toll addiction takes on the body. He put me on a strict regimen of diet, enzymes, and homeopathy. Celery juice, for example, became a daily staple because of its benefits for the liver—an organ that takes a massive hit from years of drug use. Recovery wasn't just about fixing the physical damage but pairing that progress with emotional support at every stage.

I was lucky to find a doctor who shared my spiritual beliefs, blending physical treatment with emotional guidance. He reminded me of my progress when I felt discouraged and helped me see the bigger picture. For those without this kind of dual support, I strongly recommend seeking out both a therapist and a coach who specialize in addiction recovery. And don't settle. If the connection doesn't feel right, keep looking until you find someone who aligns with you. The relationship you build with them is critical to your success.

One of the biggest barriers to recovery is the mindset of those around you. I can't tell you how many people doubted me, spouting negativity based on "statistics" or "facts." They'd throw numbers at me, telling me how unlikely it was that I'd succeed, and all but urged me to give up.

To those people, I say: fuck off.

Your negativity says more about your own fears and failures than it does about others. Would any great athlete or leader have achieved their dreams if they listened to people like you? When you pour your heart into something and believe in it fully, life will open doors for you. And when those doors open, those same people will dismiss your success as luck or an anomaly.

If you encounter these types of people, walk away. Don't waste your energy on them. Surround yourself with those who truly believe in you and your ability to succeed. Because at the end of the day, recovery is your journey. Only you can choose who's part of it.

## Inspiration

It's in your darkest days that the greatest need for inspiration arises. You might look for external help, but the truth is, the drive to change has to come from within. So how do you ignite that spark? How do you find something to hold onto? The greatest part about the world we live in today is how connected we are to others and their stories. Through the experiences of others, we find guidance, insight, and commonality. But the most powerful thing we can draw from them is inspiration—something that not only gives us hope but fosters belief in ourselves and a vision for our future.

When I reflect on the times I felt hopeless, there was always one common theme: I had nothing to work toward. There was no goal and no path to follow. To cope, I buried myself in activities that numbed my emotions. In a world saturated with social media and technology, it was all too easy to fall into that trap.

So when and where do we look for inspiration?

*In Times of Struggle*

We often seek inspiration when life feels impossible to overcome.

It's important to remember that no matter how unique your emotions or situation may feel, others have walked similar paths. They've faced their challenges, found their way out, and often learned from the successes and failures of others before them. This cycle of growth and support is timeless—and you might find yourself part of it, not only receiving inspiration but one day inspiring others.

For me, one of the most motivating figures is David Goggins—a former Navy SEAL, marathon runner, public speaker, and author of Can't Hurt Me. His story of overcoming immense challenges is unmatched, and his philosophy of seeking growth through suffering has always resonated with me. Goggins created an alter ego, "Goggins," who thrives in hardship, seeking suffering as a way to make all other challenges seem trivial.

This mindset isn't for everyone, but his raw truth keeps you honest. I've realized that many of my struggles came from my own weaknesses—fear, greed, and impatience. Admitting this isn't easy, but integrity—especially when no one is watching—has the power to transform your life.

*When We Lack Direction*

Inspiration also becomes essential when we're stuck in complacency, navigating life without aim. As Jordan Peterson explains, humans have always been tasked with navigating life physically and mentally, but without a destination, we end up going in circles. Without a way to measure progress, how can we truly grow?

After overcoming addiction, I threw myself into my corporate job as my primary avenue for development. The same place that had fueled my drug use became the same path I clung to, despite knowing deep down it wasn't the answer. I asked myself: Who do I want to be? The vision included fatherhood someday, but I also knew I wouldn't want that responsibility unless I was secure in my own growth.

Would my job and career path allow me to become the person I wanted to be? The honest answer was no. It might offer financial security, but not fulfillment. So I shifted my focus. That's when the idea for this book came to mind—not as a financial goal but as a starting point for something meaningful. It became about creating a foundation for personal growth and a better future for myself and those I love.

*When We Need to Create*

Creativity is one of the most powerful tools we have, yet so often it goes untapped. Marie-Louise von Franz once said that, "One of the most destructive forces is unused creative power." Every one of us has an infinite well of creativity, regardless of our personality or natural abilities. The key is finding inspiration and using it to channel your creative energy into building the life you want.

For many addicts, creativity is buried under destructive habits, numbing the ability to explore and discover healthier outlets. It takes time, effort, and sometimes painful trial and error to uncover what truly fulfills you. The satisfaction offered by drugs, technology, or other destructive patterns is always a dead-end road.

*When We Don't Feel Valuable*

In a world obsessed with perfection and status, it's easy to feel like we're not enough. We compare ourselves to others and forget that no one started where we did. No one else has lived your life or carried your unique experiences and emotions.

Start by identifying what makes you unhappy. Then ask yourself: What can I accomplish that would bring me joy?

For me, staying in a job I hated wasn't just making me unhappy— it was blocking my creativity and leaving me stuck in a cycle of dissatisfaction. I realized that if I continued down that path, I'd never be in a position to have a family or provide the stability I wanted for them. My journey toward finding happiness and meaning began with the creation of this book.

I wanted to use my setbacks and experiences to help others. It's not just about personal satisfaction; it's about building something bigger than myself—something that could inspire others to find their best selves.

The path to inspiration often begins with a question: What do I want to create? Who do I want to become? How do I want to contribute to the world? These questions guide us toward clarity and purpose. The answers might take time to discover, but the search itself is trans-formative.

Inspiration doesn't have to be grand or immediate. It can come from small, consistent steps. It's about finding what moves you, connecting with it, and letting it guide your journey forward. Whether it's through creativity, self-discovery, or seeking out the stories of others, inspiration is the key to unlocking your potential—and creating a life you can be proud of.


Into The Deep


Into the deep, I go again.

Shallow the depths, I dive at first
No fear, no doubt, no thought of the worst.
A curious need, some form of relief
Nothing there, still, something beneath.

Growing in fear, each dive I take
Aside this euphoric wave, relieving an undefined ache.
Mind pleads stop, body yearns for more
One in the same, both of subconscious implore.

Into the deep, I go again
Further now, because I can.

Light at the surface, distant and cold
The mind gone numb, no thought or control.
Memory of what was, no longer of late
No path to return, the unknown, now my fate.

Quiet and still, a now settled mind

Enlightened by darkness, this pain can now subside.
Once unknown, now a familiar fear
Acknowledged by love, the counterpoint to persevere.

Into the deep, I go again
For others now, because I can.

## Creators of our Fate

For the past few years, I've been seeing a holistic doctor whose treatments revolve around homeopathy and the frequency of cells in our body. Beyond physical healing and treating my anxiety, my doctor frequently emphasizes the energetic nature of how we live—and how that energy shapes our reality.

Most of us exist in a state of comparison, constantly measuring ourselves against others or focusing on what we lack. This sends out a vibration frequency of scarcity, and as a result, life reflects back to us more of the same: a sense of being without—without money, love, health, or happiness. Our physical bodies are hardwired for safety and survival, so even when we're unhappy, we find comfort in the familiar. This creates a cycle of repeated experiences that generate negative thoughts, emotions, and energy. Trapped in this loop, our expectations feed into our reality, and the cycle continues.

So how do we disrupt this cycle and become who we truly want to be? It begins with intention. We must live into the emotion of the experience we want to create.

Take, for example, someone who desires a romantic relationship but finds themselves alone. They might focus on their loneliness, leading to feelings of sadness, unworthiness, or self-doubt. These emotions perpetuate the cycle, keeping them stuck. But what if they instead imagined the joy and fulfillment of already having that connection? What if they felt so validated and loved that their instinct was to share that love with others?

This shift requires consciously living into the emotions of the life you want—not the one you have today, but the one you're creating for tomorrow. By practicing this regularly, we align our energy with what we desire. The universe, responding to this alignment, has no choice but to say yes. When you live as though your dreams are already realized, you invite them into your reality—because they already exist.

Jim Carrey, one of my favorite actors, is a perfect example of someone who turned adversity into triumph. Growing up, his family faced significant hardship. When Jim was in high school, his father lost his job, forcing the family into financial turmoil. To help pay the bills, Jim dropped out of school and worked as a janitor. Even with his efforts, the family lost their home and ended up living in a van. Eventually, Jim moved to Los Angeles, where he found success in the comedy circuit and landed his first television show. Over time, he became the household name we know and love. But Jim's perspective on life remains refreshingly humble and profound. He often speaks about the pursuit of happiness and the importance of action: as long as we continue moving toward what we want, opportunities will arise. The key, he says, is to immerse yourself in the process, because life is always happening—it's up to us to meet it halfway.

J.K. Rowling is another powerful example of creating a new reality. After college, she faced what she described as abject failure: a broken marriage, unemployment, and the daunting task of raising her daughter alone. Depression weighed heavily on her, and at her lowest, she even contemplated suicide. Despite these challenges, Rowling pursued her passion for writing. She spent hours in cafés crafting what would become her first book, Harry Potter and the Philosopher's Stone, while her daughter slept beside her. That one act of creation not only transformed her life but also inspired millions worldwide.

We are the architects of our worlds, whether we realize it or not. Every experience we create—good or bad—teaches us something about ourselves. Sometimes, it takes hitting rock bottom to spark the fire of divine creation within us. For others, the spark may never come. But the beauty of life is that sources of inspiration are all around us, reminding us of what's possible.

Our task is to embrace this truth and take ownership of our reality. By aligning our energy with what we desire and living into the emotions of our dreams, we can transform our lives. We are the creators of our fate. The only question is: what will you choose to create?

## Lessons Learned

We all face challenges in life, but it's the act of overcoming them that truly shapes who we are. There's value in sharing those experiences, as the lessons we learn can inspire and guide others.

Sometimes, it's only through pain and suffering that we can uncover the deeper message and find clarity.

As I worked my way out of addiction and into a space where growth and progress became possible, I kept a journal of my struggles and breakthroughs. Looking back, hindsight was always 20/20, but even then, I understood the importance of documenting the journey—long before this book became a reality.

Over time, those reflections distilled into a collection of actionable insights. They aren't intended as a replacement for the 12-step program or any established system, but rather as personal guidance that stems from lived experience. I believe these lessons have the potential to shape your own recovery process, just as they did mine.

## 1. Forgiveness

There's nothing more powerful than the ability to forgive yourself—both now and in the future. If you've made it to this point, it's because you truly desire change and are searching for the tools and inspiration to support it. Addiction isn't a puzzle to solve overnight; it's a journey filled with setbacks and failure. And here's the truth: no one's perspective matters more than your own, because only you hold the power to save yourself.

Take this moment to reflect. Forgive yourself for the mistakes of your past and recognize that those mistakes are part of a larger lesson—one you're here to experience and grow from. Accept that failure is inevitable. It's not a sign of weakness but a necessary step toward progress. When it happens, don't see it as a setback; see it as a step forward.

Without forgiveness, you'll never find the mental or emotional freedom to keep climbing. So, take a deep breath, smile, and let go of the weight you've been carrying. You deserve it.

2. *A Reality Check*

Take a moment to pause and reflect: where do you stand on the timeline of your addiction? While the journey to recovery is unique for everyone, the stages along the way often follow a similar progression: Initiation, Experimentation, Regular Usage, Dependence, Risky Usage, Addiction, and Treatment.

If you're in the earlier stages, such as Initiation or Experimentation, there's still a chance to halt the process before it deepens. If this sounds like you, the best thing you can do is take immediate action—open up to your friends or family and share what you're going through. Doing this now can potentially save you from years of struggle. Skip down to points 4-7 for guidance on how to make that step.

For those further along, it's crucial to acknowledge where you are on this timeline. Awareness is the first step toward regaining control. Reflecting on your position can spark important thoughts about your actions and what lies ahead. While it won't eliminate the risks, this self-awareness will help you make more informed decisions.

If you're not in immediate danger or crisis but are ready to start addressing your addiction, try creating a timeline for your recovery. Think about where you are today and where you'd like to be in two or three years. Then, temper those expectations with the reality that recovery—especially the long-term physical and mental aspects—often takes more time than anticipated. Consider the ripple effect on your life goals: meeting a partner, starting a family, or achieving career milestones.

Many people mistakenly think the end of addiction is marked by the day they stop using. But that's just the beginning. The mental and physical recovery process is long and layered, requiring patience and persistence. Regularly revisit this "checkpoint" to re-calibrate and ensure your expectations align with your progress. Remember, recovery isn't static—it evolves as you do.

*3. An Alternate You*

Sometimes the only way to break free from the weight of your own mind is to step into the shoes of a different version of yourself—a stronger, more resilient version you might not fully believe in yet. Even if it feels like acting, the goal is to build a version of you that can create a reality your current self might never achieve. It's about adopting a new mindset, one that allows you to experiment with new patterns of living and, in time, create new emotional responses.

Many people turn to medication as a way to gain the mental space needed for this transformation. Medication can provide a buffer from overwhelming emotions, giving you the opportunity to begin the work of creating that alternate self. But regardless of the tools you use, the journey is about intentional action and commitment.

A prime example of this concept is David Goggins, the ex-Navy SEAL, endurance athlete, author, and public speaker. Goggins lives by a relentless philosophy of embracing discomfort and turning it into strength. His success stems from a daily practice of seeking out suffering—pushing himself until the uncomfortable becomes second nature. While his method might not be suited for everyone, the underlying principle is universal: growth comes from deliberate, consistent effort over time.

Success stories don't happen overnight. They begin with small, incremental changes that build momentum, eventually leading to trans-formative shifts. There's nothing fundamentally different about you compared to those who've found success. The only question is how much you want it and how much effort you're willing to put in.

The alternate you isn't a fantasy—it's a reflection of the potential already within you, waiting to be unlocked. Start today by imagining who that person could be, and take one step toward becoming them. Each day, one step at a time, you'll move closer to a stronger, more capable version of yourself.

4. *To get clean, you need to come clean*

There is nothing more counterproductive to growth than hiding your struggles from the world. Addiction thrives in secrecy, and as long as you keep it hidden, it maintains its power over you. For years, I kept my battles a secret from nearly everyone, including my family. Part of me didn't want the ride to end, and part of me feared what might happen if I let others see the truth. Would they judge me? Would they even understand? These questions kept me locked in a cycle of silence.

But here's the truth: hiding doesn't protect you—it isolates you. And while opening up may feel terrifying, it's often the first step toward true recovery. Letting your family or friends in can be a lot for them to handle, but in the end, they'll be thankful. Why? Because you gave them the chance to help before it was too late.

I'll admit, I was incredibly scared of being honest. The idea of sharing my struggles felt like admitting failure. But in my darkest moments, desperation for an escape grew louder than my fear of being judged. That desperation became my turning point.

The first step in getting clean is coming clean. It's not about having all the answers or a fully formed plan for recovery. It's about setting a new course. Even if you have no idea what lies ahead, honesty puts you on a path toward something different— something better. It won't be easy, but it will be worth it. Take that step. Let someone in. You don't have to do this alone.

5. The meaning of it all

Throughout my life, I've often wondered about our purpose— why we're here and what drives us forward when the odds are stacked against us. When life feels like it's crumbling, where do we find the light? For some, it comes from religion, faith, spirituality, or something bigger. For others, it comes from within. But even if you feel detached from any greater force, the power to define meaning lies in your hands.

I think back to the year my father passed away unexpectedly. He was such a powerful and unique presence in my life, and I couldn't imagine the world without him. Losing him felt like losing my anchor, and I didn't know how to move forward. I convinced myself he'd always be watching over me, that he'd keep me safe from harm—my own personal angel.

But life didn't get easier. It got harder. Challenge after challenge came, stripping away everything I thought I had: my health, happiness, financial stability. I felt like I'd hit rock bottom, like there was no way out. Anger replaced grief, directed at both him and the higher power I once believed in. If he was watching over me, why was I losing everything? Why did it feel like life was punishing me?

One day, I stumbled upon a speech by David Goggins. Someone in the audience asked him what to do when all hope feels lost. His response stuck with me: "I did fuck up, and yes, I am in a horrible spot right now...but what if? What if this was all meant to happen? What if I turn this around, and in just a few years, this moment isn't just a memory but the very reason for my success?"

That single question changed a lot for me. I started to see my struggles as something more than just pain—they became potential. A path of light opened up in the same darkness I thought would consume me. Walking that path hasn't been easy. It's been full of struggle, setbacks, and hard lessons. But no matter how tough it gets, I keep going.

The meaning of my challenges, the depth of my lowest moments, is only clear now because I kept moving forward. Whatever you're facing, keep walking. You'll find that same light, and one day, the reason for your downfall may just become the foundation of your success.

## 6. Change your investments

At first, the mountain of recovery feels insurmountable. It's easy to become demotivated and fall off track, especially when your strength is running on fumes. So, what do you do? Do you give in and let the weight of it all consume you? Or do you focus on finding a way forward?

The hardest part for me was grappling with regret. I would spiral thinking about what I'd lost, how much time I'd wasted, and where I might have been if I'd made better choices. That regret became its own kind of addiction—an endless loop of self-blame that dug me into a deeper hole. But one day, something shifted. I decided enough was enough. I didn't need to have all the answers, but I needed to try something—anything—different. Even a small change in direction felt like progress.

For years, I thought of "investment" as something tied to money—something big, calculated, and dependent on resources I didn't have. But I began to realize that the most valuable investments are the ones that don't cost a dime. They require only you, and that's all you'll ever need to succeed. Start small. Invest your time in ways that generate momentum, no matter how modest the steps. Try exercise. Commit to eating better. Explore new hobbies. Take vitamins. Engage in things that rebuild you physically, emotionally, and mentally. Every little effort compounds over time.

The goal isn't just to change yourself—it's to recreate yourself into someone who inspires change in others. By investing in your growth, you remind yourself and those around you that transformation is possible. You are worthy of change. You are worthy of being a source of inspiration. It all starts with deciding to shift your focus, even for a moment, toward something better.

### 7. Creating Chaos & Obstacles

Addiction takes you to a place where your need becomes insatiable—a void you can never fill. The deeper I went, the harder it was to see any light, and I began to lose touch with the person I once was. It was a sad and isolating reality, one where addiction held all the power, and I felt completely defenseless. When I realized how far I had fallen, I knew I couldn't fight addiction on its terms. My only option was to outsmart it. I decided to play chess with the addicted version of myself, using my sober moments to create obstacles and challenges for the part of me that wanted to use.

It started small. I cut off access to money by destroying my credit and debit cards, making it impossible to buy what I needed to fuel my addiction. Sometimes, I transferred funds into accounts that took days to access, forcing a buffer between temptation and action. I even went so far as to delete my dealers' numbers from my phone so I couldn't contact them during moments of weakness.

Then I moved beyond financial barriers and started creating commitments that kept me accountable. I'd plan activities with friends, like hikes or dinners, and let them know how much I needed their support to stick to those plans. I made sure to prioritize time with people who could anchor me in sobriety rather than tempt me to spiral. Each barrier I created made life harder for the addicted version of me. At the time, I hated myself for it. When I couldn't use, I'd feel a mix of anger, frustration, and resentment. But deep down, I knew these obstacles were saving me.

This approach turned into an ongoing battle between the version of me that wanted to stay clean and the part that wanted to give in. It wasn't a linear process, and I didn't always win. But with every small victory, the narrative began to shift. I was no longer powerless—I was fighting back, one strategic move at a time.

In the end, those barriers I built during moments of clarity became the foundation for a new character in my story: the version of me that eventually won. And let me tell you, that version was worth every ounce of effort.

## 8. To the Edge and Back

Addiction thrives on a lack of control. The smallest triggers—a text, an ATM withdrawal, a stressful moment—can pull you back in, even when you swore you wouldn't. I've been there, starting the day with regret and a vow never to use again, only to find myself right back in the same cycle by evening. Dealers know this, and they exploit it. They hold the power because they have what you need, and they'll do whatever it takes to keep you coming back. That realization was sobering for me, and it became clear I needed to take some of that power back.

I started an experiment that I called "going to the edge and back." When cravings hit, I let the process unfold as it always did—but only up to the final step. I allowed myself to text my dealer, set up the time and place to meet, and even withdraw the money. I'd drive to the meeting spot, park, and let it all feel real. But then, in the last moment, I'd stop. I'd take a deep breath, turn my car around, and leave.

The first time I did this, my dealer called and texted repeatedly, confused and frustrated. But I didn't answer. I just drove home. And as I pulled away, something clicked. For the first time, I felt like I'd won a battle in this endless war. This experiment didn't magically cure me. Addiction doesn't work that way. Change isn't one monumental decision; it's a series of small, consistent choices that build over time. Some days I succeeded; others, I didn't. But each time I chose to turn back, I grew a little stronger.

Eventually, I pushed the experiment even further. I'd go through the motions, buy the pills, and then flush them down the toilet. It wasn't about wasting money—it was about proving to myself that I held the power. Slowly but surely, I was reclaiming control—not just over my dealer, but over the substance itself.

This process taught me that change doesn't happen all at once. It's messy, full of setbacks and small victories. But those small victories matter. Each one is a step toward something bigger, even if you don't see it yet.

Every time I went to the edge and came back, I was choosing myself. I was choosing hope, resilience, and the possibility of a different life. And with each choice, I was taking another step closer to change.

## 9. Putting Skin in the Game

When it comes to making a change, you have two options: keep it private or share it with others.

Keeping your efforts private has its benefits—it shields you from judgment and the pressure of public failure. If you relapse, the disappointment is yours alone to manage. However, there's a downside: without accountability, it's easier to give up. No one's watching, so there's no external reason to stay on course. Additionally, when you keep your journey private, you miss out on the opportunity to gain support and encouragement from others, which can be a powerful motivator.

On the other hand, sharing your decision to change is what I call "putting skin in the game." It's bold, risky, and vulnerable, but it can also be trans-formative. When you share your journey, you create accountability—not just to yourself but to those you've confided in. Knowing that others are rooting for you (or simply watching) can provide the extra push you need to follow through.

For me, sharing my struggles and intentions has been a game-changer. Talking openly about my addiction, my setbacks, and my victories has kept me honest. It's not just about seeking validation; it's about reinforcing my commitment to change. When I stumble, the people I've shared with are there to catch me or push me forward. Sharing also dismantles the isolation that addiction creates—it brings your battle into the light where others can support and encourage you.

That said, it's essential to be selective about who you share with. Trust is key. Open up to those you know will support you unconditionally, whether it's family, close friends, or even someone new who can offer fresh perspective without preconceived notions of who you are. The right people will see you for who you're becoming, not just who you were.

Change begins with belief—belief in yourself and in the possibility of a better life. But belief alone isn't enough. Surround yourself with people who will hold you accountable, cheer you on, and remind you why you started when the road gets tough. Put your skin in the game—it's a risk worth taking.

## 10. New Relationships

As we move through life, we inevitably leave people behind— friends, acquaintances, even family members. This can happen for many reasons, but often it's because the version of ourselves they knew is no longer who we are. Growth is a journey, and not everyone has the chance to witness it firsthand. This creates a disconnect, making it difficult for them to adjust to the person you're becoming. It's why, as mentioned in point nine, being selective about who you invite into your journey is so important.

Equally important, though, are the new relationships you build for the future. The people you meet today have also been on their own journeys of growth and change. When you connect with them, it's often because they align with who you're becoming, not who you were. These new connections support your evolution and encourage you to keep growing.

As we age, our capacity to connect expands—often in ways we don't anticipate. We become more open to relationships across all kinds of boundaries: age, background, perspective. The people who fit into this space in my life have been invaluable. They see me as I am now, as well as who I'm striving to be. They celebrate my progress and hold me accountable when needed. They are the ones I look to for inspiration because they've walked paths I admire.

Take some time to reflect on your current relationships. How many of them are with people from your distant past, and how many are newer connections? If the majority are from your past, it might be time to broaden your circle. Seek out people who align with your goals and values—people who inspire and challenge you.

Human connection is vital to personal growth, and while technology and social media are great tools for expanding your network, nothing compares to the depth and authenticity of in-person connections. Make the effort to forge new relationships that will help you grow into the person you're striving to become. These relationships will become some of your greatest assets on your journey.

## 11. Sacred Ground

Addiction has a way of stealing the joy from everything it

touches. Activities and experiences you once loved become tainted, losing their spark without the artificial glow that substances provide. After years of addiction, I found myself in a place where every aspect of my life seemed tied to the haze of being high. When I tried to stop, it was as if everything I enjoyed had turned dull and lifeless.

That's when I began to understand the concept of "Sacred Ground." For me, this meant identifying the areas of my life that were untouched by addiction and protecting them fiercely. These were activities and relationships that still held value, unsullied by the fog of my past habits.

For example, I recognized early on that certain things—like physical exercise, music, reading, writing, playing pool, spending time with my dogs, and connecting with positive friends—needed to remain sacred. These were the parts of my life that kept me grounded and gave me something to hold onto during the darkest times. They were my refuge, the places I could turn to when everything else felt out of reach.

But as I began to heal, I realized that simply protecting what I had wasn't enough. I needed to expand my sacred ground, to create new spaces and habits that could help me grow into the person I wanted to be. Activities like meditation, exploring faith, improving my diet, learning craftsmanship, and writing became critical parts of this process. These new experiences sparked a kind of excitement I hadn't felt in years—proof that recovery could lead to a richer, more fulfilling life.

Take some time to reflect on your own sacred ground. What are the areas in your life that addiction hasn't touched, or that you want to reclaim? Maybe it's a hobby, a relationship, or even a specific place where you feel safe and at peace. Recognize the value these spaces hold compared to your addiction, and protect them.

Then, think about what new sacred ground you can create. What activities or practices could help you heal emotionally, grow spiritually, or find joy in the present moment? Building these new spaces will take time, but they'll be crucial to your long-term recovery. Sacred ground is your foundation, the safe harbor you can return to as you continue to move forward.

## 12. Always There

When it comes to addiction, the possibility of relapse is something that will always exist. It's not meant to frighten you but to reinforce the importance of awareness and vigilance. Addiction is like a shadow—it may not dominate your life anymore, but it lingers, waiting for moments of weakness or complacency. Defense is your most valuable offense, and having a healthy level of fear keeps you cautious and grounded. Without that caution, it's easy to let your guard down and risk slipping back into old patterns.

It's also important to remember that your vulnerabilities as a person may extend beyond your primary addiction. Recovery is about more than abstaining from one particular substance or habit; it's about understanding the root causes of why you turned to it in the first place. Left unchecked, those same vulnerabilities can lead to other forms of escape, whether it's alcohol, gambling, compulsive shopping, or even technology. Recovery is an ongoing process of self-awareness and growth.

If you ever feel uncertain about your ability to maintain awareness, try creating a tangible reminder of your journey. Place an object in your home, car, or workspace—something that symbolizes your commitment to staying clean and serves as a quiet nudge when you need it. For me, it's a chain I wear around my neck, a tribute to my father and the lessons I've learned from his mistakes. I don't dwell on it every moment, but its presence reminds me of where I've been, where I'm headed, and the importance of staying mindful.

It's okay to feel proud of how far you've come in your recovery. Celebrate your victories, but don't shy away from acknowledging the presence of your addiction. Pretending it's gone forever won't make it disappear. Instead, honor your awareness of it and the growth you've achieved. Your addiction doesn't define you, but understanding its place in your life and addressing it with intention will ensure it never holds power over you again. This journey began with your awareness and will continue to flourish because of it.

## 13. The Triggers

Triggers are like a hidden minefield, especially during the early stages of recovery. Overcoming them is not something that happens overnight. It requires a long-term strategy of awareness, planning, and consistent execution. The first step is to identify your triggers. Start by making a comprehensive list, covering both external triggers (places, people, situations) and internal triggers (emotions, memories, thoughts). Pay close attention to how these triggers make you feel and how they might lead you toward relapse.

Begin with the "low-hanging fruit"—the triggers that are easiest to address or eliminate. For me, it started with cutting out specific places I used to frequent and distancing myself from people who had no positive role in my life. These were people who didn't uplift me, who encouraged bad habits, or whose presence made it harder for me to move forward. While this wasn't easy, the decision was in my hands, and I knew it was necessary to make progress. You can't build a better future while staying tied to people or environments that are part of your downfall.

Once you've tackled the easier triggers, move on to the emotional triggers—those feelings like sadness, depression, anxiety, stress, or anger that often pull you toward using. Addressing emotional triggers is one of the hardest parts of recovery because it requires not only awareness but also active effort to change how you respond in those moments. These emotions may not disappear, but you can learn to process them in healthier ways.

This part of the journey is rarely one you can take alone. Enlist the help of trusted family members and friends, and be honest about your triggers and your goals for improvement. Explain how they can support you—whether by holding you accountable, helping you avoid certain situations, or simply being there when you need to talk. Sometimes, the people you care about may inadvertently be part of your triggers. In those cases, having open, respectful communication about your recovery can make a world of difference.

Every step you take in recognizing and managing your triggers builds momentum. With time and practice, you'll strengthen your ability to respond to them without falling back into old patterns. It's a slow process, but each small victory adds up to significant progress, leading you further down the path to freedom.

### 14. Managing Stress

Stress is a major trigger for addiction, and how we handle it can determine whether we move forward or spiral backward. It's not just about avoiding stress but learning to coexist with it in a way that doesn't consume us. For years, I struggled with this balance, and while I'm still far from perfect, I've learned that managing stress isn't about eliminating it—it's about channeling it.

Addiction thrives in chaos. Stress creates the perfect environment for addiction to take hold, especially when we don't have healthy outlets. Early in my recovery, I realized that long-term success boiled down to consistent daily choices. These choices weren't limited to avoiding relapse but extended to my health, relationships, education, and personal growth. Each decision, no matter how small, added up over time. The more consistent I was, the easier it became to stay on track.

One of the first steps I took was identifying behaviors that negatively impacted my ability to manage stress. For me, that meant cutting out alcohol, junk food, and excessive time spent on technology. These things had become crutches, masking my deeper issues without actually addressing them. Beyond external changes, I also had to confront my internal struggles— anger, impatience, and a tendency to let stressful moments control me.

Once I started removing the negatives, I made space for healthier habits. The goal wasn't just to fill the void but to create a foundation of new routines that supported my growth. Recovery isn't just about stopping harmful behaviors; it's about building a new life where those behaviors have no place. Here are some practices that helped me transform how I manage stress:

*Juicing*: Starting my day with celery juice or green juice became a ritual. It's not just about detoxification—it's about starting my day with intention, nourishing my body, and setting the tone.

*Diet*: I shifted to a low-carbs, high-protein diet that supported my energy levels and reduced inflammation. What we put into our bodies affects our mental state more than we realize.

*Reading*: Books can be a sanctuary. Biographies remind you that struggle is universal, fiction gives you an escape, and non-fiction provided tools for growth.

*Meditation*: I explored mindfulness, transcendental meditation, and spiritual practices. This helped me create moments of calm, even on the most chaotic days.

*Exercise*: I focused on cardio-based workouts, not just for physical health but for sweating out toxins and releasing built-up tension. Movement became therapy.

*Supplements*: I worked with a professional to incorporate supplements and enzymes to support my body's recovery and reduce inflammation.

Stress isn't going to disappear, but how we respond to it can change everything. Instead of viewing stress as an enemy, I started seeing it as a signal—an opportunity to check in with myself. What's triggering this? What needs to change? The more I practiced this awareness, the more control I gained over my reactions.

Stress management isn't just about surviving tough moments; it's about building resilience so those moments don't define you. By shifting your focus to healthier habits, you give yourself the tools to face life's challenges without falling back into old patterns. You're not just managing stress—you're mastering it.

## 15. Detoxification: Reclaiming Your Body

Your body has endured years of toxins—not just from addiction, but also from poor diet, alcohol, stress, and the pollutants in your environment. Detoxification isn't just a buzzword; it's a process of renewal, one that requires patience and dedication. Imagine your body as an onion, with layers of accumulated toxins and emotions that have built up over time. As you peel back those layers, it's not just physical cleansing—it's emotional too. You might experience waves of sadness, bursts of happiness, or even anger, as your body and mind let go of what's been weighing you down.

So, where does detoxification begin? It starts with your liver. This powerhouse organ is your body's main filter, working tirelessly to remove toxins and support countless other functions essential to your health. Whether it's alcohol, processed foods, or harmful bacteria, your liver is constantly breaking down and eliminating what doesn't belong. It also produces critical substances like bile, which helps convert fat into energy, and albumin, which carries hormones and nutrients throughout your body. When your liver is functioning at its best, you'll notice the difference: clearer skin, a less bloated stomach, increased energy, and sharper mental clarity.

Detoxing your body isn't about quick fixes or trendy cleanses— it's about sustainable, deliberate choices that restore balance over time. Below are steps to help guide you through the detoxification process:

Hydration is Key: Start with the basics: drink plenty of water, ideally with a squeeze of fresh lemon. Lemon aids digestion, supports liver function, and helps your body flush out toxins. Staying hydrated is essential for every system in your body to function optimally.

Nourish with Liver-Friendly Foods: Incorporate foods known to support liver health into your diet. Broccoli, garlic, citrus fruits, spinach, and avocado are excellent choices. These foods contain antioxidants and nutrients that help your liver work more efficiently.

Juicing for the Win: Add celery juice or green juices to your routine. Celery juice, in particular, has been celebrated for its ability to support liver function and reduce inflammation. Start your morning with a glass on an empty stomach to kick-start your day.

Ditch the Harmful Stuff: Remove fatty, fried foods, alcohol, and unnecessary medications from your diet. These burden your liver and slow its ability to cleanse your body. Focus on clean, whole foods that fuel your recovery.

Incorporate Targeted Supplements: Supplements like turmeric, milk thistle, and dandelion root can support liver detoxification. Vitamins A, C, D, and E, along with minerals like calcium and zinc, help repair and protect your cells. Work with a healthcare professional to tailor the right combination for your needs.

Sweat it Out: Exercise isn't just for your mind—it's a crucial part of detoxification. Cardio-based activities that make you sweat help your body eliminate toxins through your skin, one of its largest detox pathways.

Practice Mindful Breathing: Detoxification isn't only physical; your emotional health matters too. Deep breathing exercises can help calm your nervous system, reduce stress, and improve oxygenation in your body.

Cold Water Therapy: Cold showers or baths stimulate circulation and reduce inflammation, supporting your body's natural detox processes. This practice may also help strengthen your resilience, both mentally and physically.

Commit to Consistency: Detoxification isn't an overnight fix.

The real progress happens through small, consistent changes over time. Stay committed to these practices, and let the results unfold gradually.

Remember, detoxification is more than just cleaning up what's on the inside; it's about creating an environment—both physically and emotionally—where your body and mind can heal. You are reclaiming your health, one intentional step at a time.

## A Life Long Journey

What does life look like beyond overcoming addiction?

The answer starts with a simple yet profound question: do you believe addiction is forever? For some, acknowledging that addiction will always be a part of them is not only safe but healthy. Keeping your guard up, remaining aware of your triggers, and recognizing the vulnerabilities that might lead you down dark paths are powerful tools for staying on track. While we grow stronger over time, life has a way of testing us. Under the right circumstances—stress, loss, or even celebration—old temptations might resurface. Nothing is guaranteed, and no matter how sure we are of our strength, the truth is we can't always predict how we'll respond. Sometimes, the only way to find out is by living through it.

If you're someone who no longer wants to identify as an addict, that's okay too. But consider this: could your experience be a light for others? Whether it's your children, family, or friends, sharing what you've learned might be the most meaningful way to move forward. Addiction taught me that life is experienced through emotion and perspective. Today, I'm more aware of how I respond to moments of stress or excitement. I've come to see that nearly all my mistakes—past and present—stem from fear, greed, or impatience. And I didn't just learn this from my own struggles but also from witnessing my father's life choices.

None of us are perfect. While we must be held accountable for our decisions, forgiveness is the key to growth. That forgiveness needs to come from others, yes—but also from yourself. Forgiveness gives you the space to reset, to move forward, and to let go of the weight of guilt. Mistakes are inevitable, and you will make them again. The important thing is to give yourself the breathing room to recover and keep going.

After all, you are the creator of your journey. Let it be a life full of chaos, lessons, and growth—an inspiring story for others to see and learn from.

# THE END

"What lies behind us and what lies before us are tiny matters
compared to what lies within us."
- Ralph Waldo Emerson -

The end of our battle with addiction is never truly final.
Some of us may hold on to the memory of the last time
we ever used, while for others, it's a gradual process built
on patience, persistence, and forgiveness. But before we reach that
final act—before the curtains close on this chapter of our lives—we
must face some of the hardest hurdles of the entire journey. Even
before the climb out begins, we have to reach that pivotal moment
where we decide we've had enough.

While many find their way out, there are just as many—if not more—
who don't. A life lost to addiction is often viewed as a tragic waste,
but perhaps it doesn't have to be. Each loss, as painful as it is, can
serve as part of the reason we choose to live, to keep going, and to
share our stories. Our lessons, our experiences, and our hard-earned
wisdom are the most valuable gifts we can offer to future generations.
By doing so, we honor those who didn't make it and provide hope
for those still searching for their way out.

## One Last Penny

*My mind is numbI feel no pain, I feel no joy*
*Oblige me now please, real McCoy*
*One last try, I swear I don't lie*
*Please hold me over til' I'm ready to die*
*In time I'll be better, I promise you'll see*
*Just a while longer, I'll soon be me*
*In time I'll make good, I promise you'll see*
*Just one last penny, I swear this ain't me*
*In time I'll stop, I promise you'll see*
*Just one last high, I'll soon be free..*

It's a dark and haunting image, looking back at what consumed me during the worst days of addiction. Whatever was left of me at that time wasn't much, certainly not enough to fight back. And the truth is, I didn't want to fight it most of the time. Sure, I despised it—I hated it during withdrawals, in those regret-filled mornings when the haze started to lift—but deep down, I fed it willingly. What lived inside me then was insatiable, something that could never be satisfied no matter how much I gave.

I remember those nights, alone in a fog of euphoria, sensing that something else was there. I felt its presence most vividly in the middle of the night when I woke up from restless sleep. It was like a shadow, a creature I couldn't see but knew was there. Over time, I began to acknowledge its existence. Real or not, it felt tangible to me, as if I'd developed some twisted relationship with it. It reminded me of how I feel about my father's presence today—only this wasn't comforting. The only way to rid myself

168

of it was to starve it, to take away what it desired most: me.

The depths we'll go to feed our desires are nothing short of remarkable. It's like setting a bar for yourself, but in reverse— a progressive, self-destructive lowering of standards. Each time you surpass the last low, you're shocked, but it becomes your new baseline. You keep going because the experience—the high—feels worth the sacrifice. And at first, the sacrifices seem manageable. Your money, your possessions, maybe a little of your dignity. But then the bar sinks lower. You start taking from others: your family, your friends, anyone in your path. What began as self-destruction becomes collateral damage.

Eventually, you reach a point where every high feels like it must be earned. It's no longer easy, and there's no pretense of control. Every hit, every moment of release is bought at a greater and greater cost. You dig deeper, past the image of who you once were, past the achievements and possessions that once defined you. You dig through rock bottom until there's nothing left but the raw truth of what you've become. You take from the same world that raised you, using any blessing left in exchange for just one more moment of escape. At this stage, all you're buying is time. And trust me, time is all you have left.

If progression holds true—if the addiction takes everything and leaves you with nothing—what lies beyond the dirt you keep digging? For most, it's a pulse, a raw nerve that holds the truth of who you are and why you're in pain. You reach the part of yourself that can't be numbed, hidden, or sacrificed. And when you hit that point, there are only three paths forward: death, change, or life. There's no masking it anymore. You're forced to choose.

## Last High

> *I swear, this is the last time...*
> *I swear, THIS is the last time.*
> *I swear, this IS the last time.*
> *I swear, this is the...last...time.*

How many times have you told yourself you were done? For most of us, it's a broken record—a promise we make to ourselves, a bargaining chip we use to bridge the guilt we feel with the world we can't let go of. It's not a lie, but it's not the truth either. It's a door we keep in our line of sight, saying we'll walk through it eventually, while knowing we're not ready yet. That distant thought of "one day" becomes a fleeting comfort, a way to assure ourselves the chaos is only temporary.

At some point, though, you start to revisit that thought of the exit more often. That's when things begin to shift. Even if you've tried to walk through that door before and failed, don't be too hard on yourself. Every attempt is a step forward. Each time you've reached that crossroad and faltered, it's added to a foundation of progress. Yes, those moments come with guilt and disappointment, but each one also represents a time you battled with your emotions. And no matter the outcome, every battle strengthens your ability to fight again.

It's important to remember that no matter how far you've fallen or how much you've numbed yourself, the core of who you are is still there. The person you were before addiction, the one who found joy and meaning in life's natural highs—that person is still alive inside you. Addiction might have taken control of your body, your habits, and even your sense of identity, but none of those things are permanent. They're changeable. They don't define you.

Think back to the years before addiction took hold. For most of us, that's 15-20 years of growth, challenge, and reward. Real moments of joy, warmth, and connection. Addiction, in comparison, is only a fraction of your life, no matter how all-consuming it feels now. Do you really believe that a few years of addiction can outweigh decades of who you were? The answer is no—it can't. But to make that truth a reality, you have to start reinvesting in yourself.

Even if it's just a little at a time, treat this process like an investment. Every small step—whether it's a better habit, a healthier choice, or just showing yourself kindness—is a deposit into the future you're building. These steps will form a protective barrier against the demons that want to pull you back. Life isn't supposed to be 10% struggle and 90% reward; that's the lie addiction sells us. Life is about balance—50% struggle, 50% reward—and it's that balance that makes the good times truly good.

People often ask, "When was the last time you used?" It's a question loaded with meaning, as if the date itself is proof of recovery. Personally, I can't recall the exact day, because it wasn't about drawing a line in the sand for me. My recovery wasn't one decision; it was a process. It was about taking steps, failing, forgiving myself, and trying again. I didn't fixate on the end goal—I celebrated the small wins along the way. And eventually, those small wins began to outweigh the losses.

Yes, there were moments I still used as a form of "celebration," but even those began to lose their power. The high wasn't the same, and chasing it became more exhausting than fulfilling. Tolerance rises, and the options narrow: increase the dose, find something stronger, or face the cold reality that the path only leads to death. The truth is, as bad as things feel now, continuing down this road only makes it worse. Wherever you stand today, it can get worse.

But it can also get better.

The fear of letting go—of never experiencing that "party" again—is a natural part of this process. You mourn the loss of what addiction gave you, even as you know it's destroying you. At the same time, you fear a future where you'll have to face life raw, without the crutch you've leaned on for so long. It's hard to believe you'll ever feel good again. And that's where belief becomes the most important thing: belief in your decision, belief in your future, and belief that you will be okay.

Change doesn't happen all at once, but time has a way of transforming everything—if you let it. Believe in yourself enough to give time a chance. That belief will be the foundation of the life waiting for you beyond addiction.

## Last of You

Over time, addiction strips away parts of you, layer by layer. In the beginning, youth is on your side—you can take the hits and still believe there's time to course correct. Even as the years go by, you may convince yourself that change is still possible. But with each passing year, the weight of what's been lost grows heavier. The addiction tightens its grip, growing in purpose and power, because facing the truth feels unbearable. The thought of the strength it will take to change—and the time required to regain even a fraction of yourself—can seem impossible to confront.

Your family, friends, and loved ones cling to the idea of who you used to be. They ask themselves, "How do I get my child, parent, friend, or partner back? Will they ever be the same?" The answer is both simple and difficult: the old you is gone, and they're not coming back. That doesn't mean you're lost forever, though. It means you're evolving into someone new—a version of you forged by both the pain and the perseverance it takes to survive this journey.

How your loved ones handle your addiction is important, but so is how you respond to their perceptions. You don't owe anyone your recovery—it's a process you're undertaking for yourself. Still, if their opinions matter to you, the best thing you can do is press forward and let them witness your growth. And don't worry about how perfectly it unfolds. Recovery isn't a series of checkpoints where you have to hit a milestone to prove your worth. It's about small victories, building one success on top of another until they become the foundation of a better life.

The past will call to you—it always does. It's so easy to get stuck replaying old memories, reliving mistakes, and wishing you could rewrite history. Maybe it's because those memories feel like the last connection to who you were before addiction took hold. Or maybe revisiting the past feels like a way to learn from it and avoid making the same mistakes. But here's the truth: living in the past doesn't serve you. If emotions are a key part of this process—and they are—then you have to stop looking at the past with regret and the future with fear.

Instead, redefine the past. Find meaning in your experiences that supports the life you're working toward. Use those lessons as building blocks for who you want to become. And as for the future? Live into it while staying present. Whatever emotions you associate with the version of yourself you want to be—joy, peace, confidence—start feeling those now. Don't wait for the external reality to change before you allow yourself to feel good. That old saying, "fake it until you make it," needs a re-frame: "feel it until it happens."

If you can visualize the ideal version of yourself, lay out the details. Hold that vision close and work toward it daily. One of Tony Robbins' best quotes is, "Most people overestimate what they can do in a year, but underestimate what they can do in five." Don't let the steep hills in front of you obscure the view of what lies beyond them. It will be worth it, but you have to start with belief—belief in your purpose, belief in your strength, and belief that you're capable of becoming someone even better than the person you were before.

## Last Chance

The thought that it's too late—too late to turn back, too late to change, too late to become who you were or who you want to be—is one of the cruelest lies we tell ourselves. It's a way of depriving our minds of the possibility for greatness, as if our past decisions have permanently chained us to the dark places we've been. Most of us are so harsh on ourselves, relentlessly revisiting thoughts of guilt, regret, and self-blame. It's no wonder that we attract difficulty into our lives and then wonder why.

Here's the thing: we do have the power to create the life we desire—not through some magical notion of manifestation, but through consistent thought, positive emotion, and actionable effort. When we align those three, it's just a matter of time before the results catch up.

The lie of "too late" is often tied to the fear of wasted time. When I think about all the opportunities I've wasted and the years lost to addiction, anger, and grief, it's easy to feel nauseous. But letting those ten wasted years destroy the next ten is a choice I refuse to make. After my dad passed in 2020, I had this strange belief that life was going to get better—not because I was doing anything to make it better, but because I thought I was owed something. I had this warped idea that losing my dad was like paying some kind of emotional debt, and that better days were now guaranteed to follow.

I couldn't have been more wrong. Life only got harder. Over the following months and years, I spiraled further. I carried anger everywhere, believing life was happening to me. I became a battering ram, meeting every moment of resistance with frustration and bitterness. I'd think, "See? Life is just a relentless string of bad things happening to me. What's the point?" Over time, that mindset shaped my reality. The anger fueled poor habits—terrible diet, too much alcohol, isolation, and strained family relationships. I was stuck in a cycle of negativity, and I didn't even realize that my own thoughts were reinforcing it.

But eventually, I hit a wall. I couldn't keep living that way, and I knew something had to change. I was tired of fighting life on my own terms and losing every time. For me, the shift came when I finally sought answers outside myself. The first thing I turned back to was this book—the very project I thought I'd lost for good. Something about it kept pulling at me, a reminder that this wasn't the end. That higher power I'd spent so much time resisting? It was guiding me, even when I didn't realize it.

If you're in a similar place, feeling like this might be your last chance, let me tell you: it's not. It never is. Take a moment to breathe and absorb that thought. Then remember that this life has a plan—not just for you, but for everyone who crosses your path. We're all connected, learning and growing through one an-other's experiences. If we all gave up, if we all thought it was too late, the cycle of inspiration and growth would come to a halt.

That's what keeps me going—the idea that my story, my strug-gles, and my growth could spark something in someone else. Like a ripple spreading across a still pond, each story touches another, creating waves of change far beyond what we can imagine. That connection is what matters most—it's bigger than any object, status, or temporary victory. It's a link to something greater than ourselves.

## Last Year

The final year of addiction is often a chaotic blur, a whirlwind of mistakes and failures that stack higher than ever before. Each misstep feels heavier, compounding the weight of the last. Eventually, the constant toll leads to that breaking point—a moment of clarity where you think, "I've had enough." You begin to realize there's not much left to lose other than yourself, and that recognition is what starts to shift things. By this time, friends and family have likely grown tired of your behavior. Their patience, stretched thin over the years, is now worn to the breaking point. You might notice they've stopped trying to save you. It's not that they don't care, but they've come to accept that this battle is yours to fight. That realization can hit hard. It's no longer about doing this for them; you start making changes for yourself because no one else can carry that weight anymore.

The final year isn't just about making the "right" decisions—it's about seeing life differently. It's as if the fog of addiction begins to lift, revealing a reality you couldn't see before. That clarity brings with it a reckoning. You're forced to confront just how far back you've set yourself. It's humbling, even terrifying, to realize the amount of work it will take not just to recover but to sustain your recovery long-term. That fear is a good thing. It's a guide, a reminder to avoid the paths that led you here. After years of numbing yourself to emotions, fear can become a compass, steering you toward better choices. But it's not just fear—it's also about finding new sources of motivation, new reasons to push forward.

The last year is often marked by efforts to rebuild relationships and regain trust. For many, this is one of the hardest parts. Addiction destroys trust, sometimes beyond repair. Those you care about might see your attempts at recovery as yet another fleeting promise, another selfish act to buy time before the next relapse. It's not easy to change their perception, especially when they've been burned before.

If you're serious this time, you'll have to put skin in the game. You'll need to make real commitments and follow through. Start small—reconnect with people who matter, the ones who haven't completely given up on you. Let them see that you're trying, not with words but with actions. Call them. Show up. Keep them informed about your progress. Attend the outings you've missed, even if they stopped inviting you a long time ago. These little steps may seem insignificant, but they add up.

The most important thing to understand is this: people want to see improvement. They don't expect perfection, but they want to feel like their hope isn't misplaced. Let your growth be a gift to them. Let them see it and feel it. Over time, your progress will rebuild the bridges you've burned. It won't happen overnight, but if you keep moving forward, it will happen.

So, ask yourself—are you serious about this? If you're not, the cycle will continue, and you'll fall back into old patterns. And this time, the fallout will likely include not just your own pain but the disappointment of those who dared to believe in you again. But if you are serious, then you have to go all in. Write a list of commitments—not just for yourself but for the people who still believe in you. Share that list with them. Be accountable. Commit to calling, checking in, and showing up consistently. These small actions might feel tedious, but they'll prove that you're not just talking about change—you're living it.

In the end, the greatest impact you can have is through your actions. Let your growth speak for itself. Whether you're rebuilding trust with family, reconnecting with friends, or simply trying to stay the course, every small improvement matters. Let your recovery be your redemption story—not just for yourself but for the people who've been watching and waiting for you to find your way back.

## Last Chapter

Day after day, with every withdrawal or desperate scheme to scrape together enough for drugs, it felt like I was digging myself a deeper grave. The hole seemed bottomless, and honestly, I didn't have plans to stop. Even when the thought of stopping crossed my mind, the pain I'd caused myself was so overwhelming it felt impossible not to numb it. What started as a thrill—the chase, the high, the game—slowly morphed into something bleak. I found myself sitting in my car on random streets, restlessly waiting for my dealer to call. By then, the only thing I actually enjoyed was the brief relief from withdrawal and self-loathing. The "fun" was long gone.

When you're younger, addiction can feel like a reckless game you're somehow winning. But as the years stack up, youth slips through your fingers, and the game isn't cool anymore. You're not a player; you're just another addict in need, willing to do whatever it takes to keep going. That realization hit hard. With every regret-filled day, the voice in my head—the one I'd buried under years of use—got louder. At first, I ignored it. I had the time, the resources, and the arrogance to keep pushing it aside. But life has a way of breaking you down. It became harder to drown out that voice, and the more I ignored it, the worse things got. That worsening wasn't some cosmic punishment—it was a force trying to push me to my breaking point, trying to wake me up.

Eventually, I hit a threshold. It wasn't a dramatic, life-changing moment. It was a slow, agonizing shift. There were moments where, for the first time, I chose not to use. At first, they were rare, but they started to happen more often. One day, I woke up and realized that something within me had shifted—a spark of light was flickering, battling against the darkness. That darkness, the addiction, wasn't gone. It was still strong, still clawing at me. But now, there was resistance, and every choice I made fed one side or the other.

Addiction convinces you that it's your identity. Every lie, every bad choice, every moment spent using reinforces the belief that you are an addict and nothing else. Admitting that truth is important in recovery, but eventually, that label becomes a weight you don't need to carry anymore. Yes, remembering where you've been is critical—it keeps you grounded, keeps you from slipping back. But living in the constant mindset of being an addict can keep you tethered to the past, to the darkness.

At some point, you have to shift your perspective. It's not about fighting to prove you're not an addict anymore. It's about living into the light that's starting to grow within you. You don't have to see the end of the tunnel to know you're moving in the right direction. Early on, the darkness surrounds you so completely that giving into it feels like second nature, like there's nothing left to lose. But as that light grows brighter, every step forward feels like real progress. It's not just about surviving anymore—it's about creating a life worth living.

Your journey isn't going to be linear. There will still be missteps, moments where the darkness tries to pull you back. But those moments don't define you. What defines you is the choice to keep moving forward, to let the light within you grow stronger. Every small win, every moment of resistance, every step forward is proof: the person you thought you'd lost is still in there, and they're waiting to come back to life.

## KEY TAKEAWAYS

FOR THE ADDICTS:

**Your identity is not your addiction.** The person you were before addiction is still within you, waiting to be rediscovered and nurtured.

**The process isn't linear.** Missteps and setbacks are part of the journey. Celebrate small wins and use them to build momentum.

**Light and darkness coexist.** Recovery is about strengthening the light within you, even while the darkness still lingers.

**Re-frame your past.** Look at your history not with regret but as a foundation for growth and lessons to carry forward.

**Reinvest in yourself.** Treat recovery like an investment. Every small step builds a protective barrier against relapse.

**Believe in your future.** Even when it feels impossible, trust that time and effort will lead to a better version of yourself.

**Fear can guide you.** Feeling fear again is natural and healthy—it can help steer you away from old patterns.

**You don't need to see the finish line to move forward.** Focus on the small steps in front of you. Progress happens one choice at a time.

**Healing takes time.** The damage caused by addiction won't be undone overnight. Be patient with yourself as you rebuild.

**Reconnect with your emotions.** Embrace joy, sadness, and everything in between as part of living fully and authentically.

FOR FAMILY & LOVED ONES:

**The old version of your loved one may not return.** Understand that recovery creates a new version of them, shaped by their experiences.

**Recovery is their responsibility.** While support is vital, the process of recovery ultimately lies in the hands of the addict.

**Trust takes time to rebuild.** Be patient and allow their actions, not just words, to show their commitment to change.

**Celebrate progress, not perfection.** Look for small signs of improvement and acknowledge their effort without expecting immediate transformation.

**Avoid guilt and blame.** Addiction is complex and often beyond anyone's control. Let go of any sense of responsibility for their choices.

**Encourage accountability.** Help them take ownership of their actions and their path forward without rescuing them from consequences.

**Focus on open communication.** Maintain honest, empathetic conversations that foster trust and understanding.

**Seek support for yourself.** Whether through therapy, support groups, or trusted friends, ensure you have resources to navigate this journey.

# THE AFTERMATH

"Breaking is easy, healing is the real challenge."
- Michael R. Duryea -

## Physical Impact

Detoxification is the first major hurdle any addict must face on the road to recovery. Over time, substances build up in the body, starting with the liver, which becomes overloaded as it processes toxins. This buildup doesn't leave overnight—detox is a long, grueling process, with the initial phase being the most physically and emotionally challenging. However, even after the immediate detox, the body's recovery process stretches on for months, even years, as it works to heal and re-balance.

Your body's detoxification system is a complex network of organs, each with a specific role. The liver and kidneys are the main filters, breaking down toxins and preventing them from wreaking havoc elsewhere in your body. Your skin, lungs, digestive tract, and lymphatic system also play supporting roles in expelling waste and maintaining balance. If any part of this system isn't functioning well, the ripple effect can lead to a wide range of physical and mental health issues.

## The Reality of PAWS

Post-Acute Withdrawal Syndrome (PAWS) is an umbrella term for the lingering symptoms that persist long after the initial detox. For opiate addiction, these symptoms span a spectrum of physical and mental challenges, ranging from muscle aches and fatigue to mood swings and intense cravings. PAWS often blindsides recovering addicts, as many don't realize how long this phase lasts—or how permanent some changes can feel. While it's true you may never be exactly the same, the good news is that with time, effort, and care, you can drastically reduce the intensity of these symptoms. What's left are small scars— reminders of where you've been, but also proof of how far you've come.

## Facing the Root Cause

One of the most difficult, but necessary, parts of recovery is confronting what led you to addiction in the first place. Without identifying and addressing this root cause, the risk of relapse looms large. This work requires both proactive steps, like therapy and lifestyle changes, and reactive strategies to deal with triggers as they arise.

For me, the biggest demon I've had to face is anxiety. Since childhood, I've woken up with an unshakable sense of dread, as if something terrible was about to happen. At the time, I didn't know it was anxiety—I just thought it was normal. Growing up, I pushed through social situations, presentations, and academics, all uphill battles against this invisible force. As I entered the corporate world, my anxiety escalated into full-blown panic attacks. Instead of seeking help, I stumbled upon opiates, which masked my symptoms and gave me a false sense of control. But that relief came at a cost. The stress of corporate life, which I hated with every fiber of my being, only fueled my reliance on substances. Eventually, I realized I had to take my anxiety seriously and began exploring real solutions.

While anxiety has been my primary struggle, I know depression is a significant battle for many recovering addicts. Unlike anxiety, which pushes you into overdrive, depression feels like a heavy blanket smothering your ability to function. It can rob you of motivation, isolate you, and, in the worst cases, lead to thoughts of suicide. I've been fortunate to avoid the depths of depression, but I've witnessed its devastating impact on others.

One of the most inspiring resources I've come across is the You Rock Foundation, founded by one of my brother's closest friends. They use music as a lifeline for people battling depression, providing a safe haven and a sense of connection. Their interviews with musicians like Corey Taylor (Slipknot) and Jonathan Davis (Korn) highlight that even the most seemingly untouchable people face these struggles. It's a reminder that no one is alone, and there is always hope.

No matter what drove you to addiction—whether it was anxiety, depression, trauma, or something else—recovery means addressing those underlying issues head-on. And how you go about it is your decision. Whether it's therapy, support groups, or medical treatment, what matters is that you choose a path that helps you heal without returning to self-medication.

Progress takes time, and setbacks are inevitable. But as long as you stay committed to growth, you will continue to make progress—physically, emotionally, and mentally. You've already come so far. Hold on to that momentum, and know that an incredible future is waiting for you. Don't give up. You're capable of so much more than you think.

## Mental Battles

Recovery from addiction isn't just about breaking physical dependence—it's a mental battle that requires uncovering and addressing layers of unresolved emotions, trauma, and ingrained habits. For me, the emotions that surface during this journey have often left me questioning: Are these feelings rooted in my past, or are they the result of what I've put my body through? In truth, it's likely both. Unprocessed anxiety or childhood trauma can dictate our emotional responses, while long-term physical effects of addiction can amplify those emotions in ways that feel overwhelming.

If you're not willing to do the work and uncover the root causes of your feelings, they'll control your daily life. Your reactions will be shaped by triggers and sensations you don't fully understand. This lack of awareness creates a warped approach to life, where you bend around the weight of your emotions instead of clearing them out and walking a straight path.

For me, stress management plays a pivotal role in navigating each day. Each experience tests my ability to either emotionally react or consciously respond. I'll admit I'm far from perfect, but I try to land on the right side of things as much as possible. What influences my success often comes down to two factors: my awareness of my emotions in the moment and the intention I set for the day. Meditation has been a powerful tool in helping me achieve this balance. While I'm not always consistent with the practice, when I return to it regularly, the impact is undeniable. It helps me process and release the clutter of thoughts that fill my mind, creating space for clarity, creativity, and stillness.

I'm forever grateful to my brother for introducing me to Transcendental Meditation (TM). It's a tool that's become an integral part of my life. When practiced consistently, it's like a reset button that allows me to approach challenges with a calmer, more centered mindset.

One of the scariest aspects of my journey has been dealing with panic attacks. The first one I ever experienced was about four years into my career. It happened during a casual one-on-one networking meeting with a manager on a team I was interested in joining. Looking back, there was no logical reason for me to feel nervous—I wasn't even aware of any anxiety leading up to it. But that's the thing about panic attacks—they aren't necessarily tied to the immediate situation. They're often the result of unprocessed emotions building up over time. When the strain becomes too much, it manifests physically, mimicking symptoms of a heart attack or stroke.

The aftermath of a panic attack can be just as concerning as the attack itself. Over time, the strain on your parasympathetic nervous system—the part that helps calm you down—can weaken, making it harder to regulate stress. Reflecting on my childhood, I suspect I experienced mild panic attacks without realizing what they were. If you think you might be experiencing panic attacks or similar symptoms, don't ignore them. See a doctor to rule out any underlying health issues and get baseline tests like blood-work or an EKG for your heart. If everything checks out, take it as a sign to address your stress levels and emotions through meditation, therapy, or other forms of self-care.

## The Role of Childhood Trauma

A significant number of addictions are rooted in childhood experiences. While the word "trauma" may sound dramatic, it encompasses a wide spectrum of events. Even seemingly mild experiences can have a profound impact on a child's developing mind. Without proper guidance or support, we're left to assign meaning to these events on our own. Over time, these meanings shape our beliefs, strengths, and weaknesses, which in turn influence the choices we make—or avoid making.

Taking the time to reflect on your childhood and explore the beliefs you've carried forward is a powerful step in recovery. By doing this work, you can start to rewrite the narrative, gaining control over decisions that might otherwise be made on autopilot.

## Handling Cravings and Temptations

In the weeks, months, and years after overcoming addiction, cravings and temptations will inevitably arise. They may seem to come out of nowhere, but they're often triggered by stress or struggle. Instead of fearing these moments, look at them as opportunities to validate how far you've come. They're proof that you've entered a new chapter where you have the power to choose.

One of the most effective tools I've found for managing cravings is writing. When a wave of emotion or temptation hits, I put pen to paper and let the thoughts flow. Writing creates a space between feeling and action, giving me a chance to process what's happening instead of reacting impulsively. Afterward, I engage in an activity that separates me from the cycle—like going for a run, hiking, or even just stepping outside for fresh air. These moments of intentional action help break the old patterns that once dictated my choices.

## Letting Go of Regret

One of the toughest mental hurdles in recovery is grappling with the time and opportunities lost to addiction. It's easy to fall into the trap of wondering who you could have been if only you'd chosen a different path. But the truth is, life doesn't come with guarantees. Even if you hadn't struggled with addiction, there's no telling what other challenges might have arisen. Maybe you would have found the love of your life and built the perfect family—or maybe that relationship would have ended in heartbreak.

What's important is to stop judging yourself for the decisions that set you back and start focusing on the ones that brought you to this moment. The past doesn't define you, but the choices you make today will shape the future. Don't waste the opportunity you have now to create something better. Use your story—your struggles, lessons, and victories—as a source of hope for those still searching for their way out.

You've come so far. Be the light that inspires others to believe in their own strength.

## The World and You

There will be moments when the thought of addiction re-entering your life sneaks into your mind. Take those thoughts seriously, but don't let them own you. Recognize them for what they are: echoes of your past, reminders of a path you no longer walk. It's your mind reflecting on a time when you might have fallen and reminding you, "Not anymore." Scar tissue has formed over those old wounds, and you've proven—time and time again—that no matter how bad things get, you're not going back. Don't fear approaching the edge. What lies there isn't danger but affirmation of the strength you've built.

As you move forward, friends and family might carry residual worry or fear for you. Don't let their concerns weigh you down, because they're a reflection of their experiences, not yours. Show them—through your actions, your consistency, and your joy—that they have nothing to fear. What ultimately showed my loved ones that I was truly in a better place was how I started to embrace life again. In the depths of my addiction, I could only take things one day at a time. But when I began to plan for the future, set goals, and share my excitement with them, their confidence in me grew. I learned to appreciate the small moments, to celebrate the simple joys, and to live for the opportunities ahead rather than dwell on what was lost. Remember those who didn't make it, but don't let the weight of that sorrow hold you back from living into the future.

You may need to rebuild connections with friends you drifted away from during your addiction. At first, I was afraid those friends wouldn't want to reconnect, that the bond we once shared had been severed. But here's the truth: real friendships are resilient. True friends can be apart for years and pick up right where they left off. If, for some reason, a friendship doesn't reignite, that's okay too. Not every connection is meant to last forever. Focus on the ones that do, and nurture them by being consistently present for the important moments in their lives. Be the friend who supports their growth, who uplifts them as they strive toward their goals.

As people grow older, they naturally gravitate toward those who inspire and support them. Become that person. Let your presence in their lives reflect the wisdom and strength you've gained through your recovery.

## Shifting the Spotlight

Addiction often places you at the center of attention, intentionally or not. Your struggles, your needs, your recovery—it can feel like the world has revolved around you. But when the spotlight dims and the curtain falls, you might find yourself feeling isolated. This is when you start to build new habits, ones that take the focus off yourself and onto others. Step outside your own narrative. Care about the well-being of others, not just as a distraction but as a way to re-engage with the world.

Giving attention to the lives of those around you does more than strengthen relationships—it also provides a sense of purpose. It allows you to see that your recovery isn't just about you; it's about the ripple effects your journey can create.

The choices you've made to reach this point have opened doors to an entire world of new relationships and opportunities. There's no such thing as time wasted, but there are wasted opportunities if you choose not to change. Deep down, you know what areas of your life need adjustment. For me, one of those areas has been my evening routine. I work a stressful job from 7 AM to 5 PM, and for years I used my evenings to work out, read, write, and spend time with friends or family. Over time, though, I slipped into a pattern of rest and passivity, scrolling through social media and avoiding invitations to go out. That comfort zone slowly weakened me, and I realized I'd stopped challenging myself outside of work.

We all deserve moments of rest, but if we want to achieve great things, we have to push beyond what's easy. For me, that meant taking on the challenge of rewriting this book and starting new projects. I also recognized the need to be a better listener, to practice patience, and to engage more deeply with the people around me.

What comes next for me isn't entirely clear, but I know it has to be something that pushes me beyond my current limits. The same goes for you. Find something so challenging, so ambitious, that the current version of yourself isn't equipped to accomplish it. Force yourself to grow, to adapt, and to become the person you need to be to achieve it. That's how you keep moving forward—not just surviving, but thriving.

# RECOVERY

"There is no greater, there is no lesser. There is only balance."
- Robert A. Monroe -

A ddiction rests on three interconnected elements: the life you lead, the pain it causes, and the substance that props you up. In the early stages of addiction, you're often unaware of the pain or the lifestyle that's fueling it. For a while, the opiates dominate, numbing you to the truth. But eventually, the cracks begin to show, and the real pain point—the source of your struggle—demands to be identified. That pain could stem from your environment, upbringing, beliefs, family dynamics, friendships, or a mix of it all.

As time goes on, the opiates lose their effectiveness. When that happens, every addict faces a crossroads: either increase the dosage or confront the underlying reason for using in the first place. This is where age and maturity often play a role. Younger people, in particular, may resist introspection. Instead of exploring their pain, they bury it further through experimentation, digging deeper into addiction and making recovery even harder to grasp.

For those willing to turn inward and explore the root causes of *their addiction, the path is challenging but transformative. This exploration can take many forms—therapy, group work, spiritual practices, or even practical self-reflection. The key is stepping outside of yourself and looking inward with honesty. The process won't deliver all the answers at once, but each step reveals new layers. Think of it as peeling back the layers of an onion; each one brings you closer to the core truth.*

*Along the way, you may experience pivotal "shifting" moments— breakthroughs of clarity that alter your course. Sometimes, it takes a subtle shift in perception to unlock a new and better version of yourself. With this newfound perspective, you start making decisions that support healthier patterns of living. As those patterns take root, they bring with them new emotions—ones that no longer require the crutch of opiates or any other substance.*

*Recovery isn't about a single revelation or decision; it's a layered, ongoing process. But with time, patience, and the willingness to look within, it's a process that can lead to real change—a life no longer dominated by addiction, but by the freedom to feel and live authentically.*

## Avoidance

Pain—it's something we all try to dodge, an experience no one willingly seeks out. Looking back, I can't pinpoint a specific moment in childhood where pain overwhelmed me, but there was always this persistent undercurrent of anxiety. Back then, I didn't even recognize it as anxiety—it was just life, and life felt like that. The real shift came as childhood faded and the weight of "responsibility" set in. For others, the source of their pain may stem from entirely different places—a culmination of experiences or a single defining moment. Regardless of how we arrive at that breaking point, most of us eventually find ourselves desperate for an escape from reality.

For many of us, drugs became that escape. We conditioned ourselves to a life of extremes—a world where we alternated between the blissful highs of euphoria and the crushing depths of withdrawal and regret. In those highs, we felt invincible, untouchable. But the lows always followed, steeper and darker than the last, until our greatest fears became reality.

This pattern of extremes is like a relentless wavelength—sharp peaks and deep valleys, with no middle ground. It's as though our minds and bodies learned to operate on two settings: survival mode or absolute relief. There was no transition, no steady rhythm, just a jarring shift between two opposing states.

Now think back to before addiction took hold, to the steady wavelength of childhood. Back then, the highs and lows weren't so severe. Our emotions, though challenging at times, transitioned more naturally. The highs were brighter because they were grounded in something real, and the lows were just parts of a gradual process, not devastating crashes. It was a healthier rhythm—one where we could trust that good would eventually follow bad, where hope wasn't a desperate wish but an underlying truth.

In addiction, we lose that rhythm. We lose faith in the process of growth and healing because the pain feels endless, and the climb out seems impossible. But the truth is, pain and beauty are two sides of the same coin. One cannot exist without the other. If we embrace this truth, we can start to see that the pain is temporary, that the waves do eventually level out, and that the tunnel does have a light at the end.

Success in recovery depends on our acceptance of where we are in the process. It's easy to see our current position as a dead end—a final, unchangeable state. But the reality is, life is always in transition. We are constantly moving through phases, stepping out of old patterns and into new ones. If we can acknowledge this truth, even for a moment, we open ourselves to the endless possibilities ahead.

When we recognize the existence of possibility, we increase the probability of change. Life doesn't have one single solution or a definitive endpoint. It's a journey, a constant evolution. The key is to stay open to it—to trust that even in the darkest times, transitions are happening, and those transitions hold the seeds of hope, healing, and growth.

## Denial

In the beginning, it can be hard to distinguish between avoidance and denial. Which comes first? Some might argue that avoidance means you've already acknowledged what you're steering clear of, making denial the precursor. But sometimes, you're not even fully aware of what you're avoiding—you just know the direction you're heading feels right, even if it's leading you astray. That's the tricky part. Whether it's conscious or not, avoidance becomes a pattern—a way of life. And whether you define it as moving toward what you desire or away from what you fear, the key is the same: recognizing that you are avoiding something, even if you don't yet know what it is.

To clarify (because, honestly, it's still unclear to me at times):

To avoid is to keep away or steer clear of something.
   To deny is to refuse to admit the existence of something.

Comparing the two, it's easy to see why denial poses a much greater threat. Denial is the ultimate roadblock, halting any process of self-improvement before it can even begin. What's more, denial often operates on layers, growing more entrenched the longer you live in it. The deeper the denial, the more opportunities you've likely passed up to break free from a destructive cycle. And yet, you keep doubling down, refusing to admit what's staring you in the face.

The real kicker? Denial doesn't just stay static—it gains strength over time. The longer you deny, the bigger the problem grows, until the consequences are impossible to ignore. Those consequences often come crashing down like a sledgehammer, another chance for reality to wake you up. Yet, despite the mounting evidence, denial convinces you that you're still in control. You cling to the illusion that you've got it handled, even as everything around you crumbles.

At this point, denial crosses into delusion—a dangerous place where you're blind to the reality of your choices. You're flying into a storm with no visibility, and the outcomes narrow to just two possibilities: rock bottom or death. That's the harsh truth, but it's also the pivotal moment where change becomes possible. Whether you hit the ground or find a way to pull up, the choice is ultimately yours. But you can't begin to make that choice until you confront the denial that's been steering your course.

## Acceptance

If denial is the roadblock to progress, then acceptance is the key to moving forward. It's the act of letting go of what you cannot change—especially from your past—so that you can live in the present and make better choices for the future. To truly accept is to surrender to everything you perceive as both within and beyond your control. The irony, of course, is that none of it was ever in your control to begin with. And part of genuine acceptance is allowing others to see your reality, because keeping it hidden only deepens your denial and avoids the consequences that are necessary for growth.

I know there's someone reading this right now thinking, "I'm going to use tonight, and I accept the risks that come with it." On the surface, that feels like a kind of acceptance, right? You're acknowledging the risks and making a decision. But it's not full acceptance—not even close. You're only considering the personal consequences that fit inside your narrow, self-centered perspective. Sure, you might get arrested, overdose, or wreck your life further, but have you thought about how your choices affect everyone else? The people who love you, who care about you, who will feel every ounce of pain you inflict on yourself as if it's their own?

Letting others in on your addiction doesn't just reduce your risk—it reduces theirs. They deserve the chance to prepare, to understand, and to protect themselves from being blindsided by the fallout of your choices. Yes, their involvement might come with concern, frustration, or even anger. But it also comes with honesty—and that honesty is what lays the foundation for real change.

I think back to the countless nights I drove to pick up, knowing full well the risks. I'd have conversations with myself, acknowledging the very real possibility of getting caught or overdosing. But I didn't care. I loved the reward more than I feared the consequences. Rarely, if ever, did I stop to think about how those choices impacted my family or friends. The only time they entered my mind was when I wanted someone to blame. My upbringing, my anxiety, my circumstances—it was all part of the elaborate, self-pitying narrative I'd created to justify my behavior.

I didn't care about myself, so how could I possibly care about anyone else? Acceptance wasn't even on my radar. And because I refused to accept my reality, I stayed stuck in cycles of avoidance and denial for years.

True acceptance isn't just about acknowledging the risks or consequences of your addiction—it's about embracing the full picture, including the impact you have on others. It's about breaking the pattern of selfishness and secrecy, and stepping into the light of accountability. Only then can you start to rebuild what addiction has taken away.

## Love

It feels almost cliche to talk about love and pain in the same breath, so I'll spare you the "you have to love yourself" speech. Not because it's not true—it absolutely is—but because that kind of love is something you'll discover within yourself in time. What I think is more immediate and tangible is recognizing how pain often stems from either a lack of love or, sometimes, an overwhelming abundance of it.

Most people are quicker to talk about the absence of love than they are to express it. It's easier to recount what you didn't have than to articulate what you might have needed. For me, there was never a lack of love growing up. My parents, especially my mom, always made sure my brother and I knew how much we were loved. Sure, there were moments of emotional fear when it came to my dad, but even then, we never doubted that he loved us deeply. When love feels absent—whether it's from others or from within—it can leave a lasting scar on how we see ourselves. This is often where the pain originates, in the gap between who we think we are and who we think we should be. "I'm ugly, overweight, poor, anti-social, sad, depressed, lonely, worried, unsuccessful." These labels aren't just thoughts; they're stories we tell ourselves over and over until they become the fabric of our reality.

What's worse is how quickly reality reinforces the narrative. "See, I was right," we tell ourselves when life inevitably mirrors back our insecurities. And in some twisted way, it feels easier to live in that frustration, to let the story play out as if it's beyond our control. But it's not. You have more agency than you realize, even when love feels distant.

On the other hand, there's an entirely different kind of pain that comes from having too much love, especially during childhood. When you grow up surrounded by warmth and security, adulthood can feel like a slap in the face. The sudden coldness of responsibility—finding a job, supporting yourself and others, dealing with the loss of loved ones—leaves you desperate for the comfort you once knew. That desperation can feel like screaming, "I'm not ready for this!" And in that moment of not being ready, getting high seems like the easiest way to hit pause.

But here's the thing: addiction doesn't just hit pause—it stunts you. Emotional growth comes to a screeching halt for as long as you're an addict. It's not just that you stop growing while you're in it; you regress. And when you finally do grow out of addiction, you're left to confront the cold reality that drove you there in the first place. Only now, it's worse, because you've added years of damage to yourself and your relationships.

The work to rebuild yourself will feel daunting. It will be harder than it would have been if you'd never fallen into addiction at all. But that's okay. That's the process you needed. That work—the time, effort, and patience it takes to heal—is the price you pay for the life waiting on the other side. And once you begin, you'll find that the love you thought you'd lost was never really gone. It's been waiting for you to catch up all along.

## Seasons of Loss

Loss comes in endless forms: life, love, relationships, identity, finances. Each form carries its own process—from the initial sting to the suffering, recovery, and eventual impact on your future. But at their core, all these experiences of loss center around three things: the past, the present, and the future.

When we make a mistake, like losing money or financial security, we dwell on the error, replaying it over and over in our minds. If we lose a loved one, we cling to memories, wondering if we could have done something differently to change the outcome. We mourn the past while projecting negative thoughts into the future, lamenting how much better things could have been. And in between those two extremes, we struggle to recover. We get trapped, sandwiched between thoughts of what we can't change (the past) and what we can't control (the future).

I've lost more than I can begin to quantify because of addiction, and I'll never get those years back. Years that could have been spent building a better life or becoming the person I always wanted to be. The money? Gone. Hundreds of thousands of dollars. My body and mind? Recoverable, yes, but perhaps not entirely. And still, I choose not to dwell on it. Why? Because focusing on what's gone only robs me of the present, the one thing I can control.

Years after I began my recovery, I moved back home to start digging myself out of the financial hole I had created. I lived there for about two years with my mom, dad, and our dogs. It wasn't where I'd envisioned myself at that stage in life, but it felt good to be home. I had a great relationship with my parents, and we made the most of our time together. One Sunday afternoon, I left the gym and answered a call from my mother. I'll never forget the sound of her screaming as she was trying to resuscitate my father. He had suffered a heart attack and passed away. Just like that, he was gone. My dad was the sun our family revolved around, and his loss left an irreplaceable void.

Not long after, I faced another devastating loss. On New Year's Eve, as I finished a glass of wine, I accidentally knocked it over my laptop. My entire book—Suburban Addict—was gone. I hadn't backed it up, and despite taking the laptop to three different data recovery companies, the damage was too severe. All my time, emotion, and effort over so many years was lost. My guiding light, the purpose that had kept me going, was extinguished. And I had no one to blame but myself.

Two years later, during the pandemic, we sold my mom's house, and she, my brother, and I moved to separate places. Around that time, the economy was booming. I made more money than I ever thought possible. But by 35, I had lost it all again, ending up broke and in debt. It felt like a cruel cycle, and I started to question my faith. Why did bad things keep happening? What had I done to deserve this? My mind oscillated between past mistakes and future fears, unable to find peace.

During that time, I realized something about my poor choices—

they all stemmed from fear, greed, or a lack of patience. Recognizing this truth helped me make better decisions moving forward, but it didn't erase the corrosive thoughts I was stuck with. So, I decided to focus on meditation and being alone with my thoughts. One evening, in the quiet stillness of my mind, I had a realization that changed everything:

No matter the challenge or obstacle, we get to choose the meaning of our experiences.

I had spent so many years beaten down by loss, letting it define me and dictate my future. But I realized I didn't have to. I could redefine everything I had gone through and find meaning in it.

One night, overwhelmed by anger and resentment, I questioned why God would allow so many bad things to happen. That night, I opened a book I hadn't touched in ages. The very first page I turned to spoke directly to my circumstances. It explained that the struggles we face—the ones that spark our rage—are often the very circumstances necessary for our inner growth. These moments, as painful as they are, awaken our spirits and draw us closer to something greater.

A week later, I had another tough day. Out of nowhere, I received an email from an unknown address. It read: "Even as the Son of Man came not to be served but to serve, and to give his life as a ransom for many." That message cemented something in me. I sat down that night and started to redefine the meaning of the losses I had endured. I realized that losing the money I had made was a blessing; I hadn't been ready for it. Whatever path I would have taken if I hadn't lost it wouldn't have included re-writing this book.

I had survived nearly a decade of addiction and come out the other side with knowledge and experience to help others. So, I re-outlined the entire book and began writing again, day by day.

It's never too late to change your future, no matter how much you've lost. Loss is inevitable, but it doesn't have to define you. What defines you is what you do with it—how you choose to interpret it, learn from it, and use it to grow. Let every setback be a step forward. Let every loss be a lesson. And let your life's purpose come from a place of service—not just to honor the best version of yourself but to support the well-being of others.

## Giving Back

The most powerful choice you can make now is to help others by sharing your experience and the lessons you've learned. Don't hide from your past or feel ashamed of what you've endured— find the light within yourself and let it shine as a beacon of hope for those still struggling. There are countless ways to give back, whether it's through attending or leading meetings, writing, joining social media groups, or volunteering at rehabilitation facilities. If helping those suffering from addiction feels too overwhelming at first, start small. Community service of any kind can set you on the right path. Sometimes, just placing yourself in spaces of activity and service allows life to connect you with the right people and experiences.

As you start giving back, don't overlook the ones who supported you from the beginning—your family. It's often easier to rebuild yourself and show the best version of who you've become to new faces. But that shouldn't stop you from also strengthening and transforming your relationships with family members. As we grow older, the dynamics of family shift. Senior members pass, and the responsibility of holding the family together gradually transitions to the next generation. To step into this role, your bonds with siblings and extended family must be strong. Remember, the well-being and actions of those at the top have a direct impact on the younger generations watching and learning from you. Be the example they need.

A recent lesson I learned came from studying monasticism. Most of us assume monks are born into their lifestyle, raised with the discipline and serenity we associate with them. But the truth is, many monks come from lives of hardship, poor decisions, and struggle. They sought refuge in monasticism and found a profound purpose in its simplicity and devotion. Their extreme commitment to abstinence from marriage, money, and worldly pleasures offers a life with very few distractions but immense meaning.

While I doubt either of us will be donning a monk's robe anytime soon, there's something we can learn from their path. Recovery, in a way, is a form of spiritual discipline. It limits some choices but opens up a world of clarity and purpose if approached with the right mindset. Our ability to simplify, focus, and commit to helping others can transform not only our lives but the lives of those around us.

One common thread among those who've overcome addiction is the discovery of a new purpose. For some, the purpose may simply be living a life free of suffering, but those who thrive understand that life without meaning feels empty. True purpose often comes from serving others.

We live in a world that constantly makes us feel like we're lacking—whether it's material possessions, status, or relation-ships. Gratitude is your antidote to this mindset. Be thankful for what you have because life can take it away in an instant. When you reflect on where you've come from, the hardships you've faced, and the battles you've fought, you'll see how far you've come.

More importantly, you'll realize how essential you are to the lives of others. Your story has the power to inspire, to guide, and to give hope. Embrace that power, and use it to fulfill a purpose greater than yourself. Because no matter where you've been or how much you've lost, your purpose has just begun.

# THE OPTIMIST

O ver the years I often heard news of someone who passed from an addiction or overdose, but it was never close to home. More often than not they were a friend of a friend, or someone we knew from our hometown or childhood. I found myself fortunate in this light, especially as someone who's personally battled addiction.

This unfortunately changed after my best friend's older brother recently passed, who was not only my older brother's best friend, but a brother and friend to me. He was more than just another statistic; he was a son, a brother, a friend – a special spirit who's laughter and love for life was pure. No matter the situation or mood, being around him made you feel better.

To quote my brother, he was a real life medicine man with a prescription for love, optimism, and fun. He was incredibly creative, and channeled this through his projects, art, and writing over the years. With the blessing of his family, these writings are shared as both a tribute to his life, and source of inspiration for those in need.

## Letting Go

I have written this in hopes of not only helping others break through their own unique challenges, but also as a medium to illustrate and better understand all of my ideas, theories and beliefs to evolve into a better person. Every chapter's underlining message was inspired by something that was going on in my life at the time it was written. I like to think that each chapter represents a piece of the puzzle that is our lives. Because there can never be another puzzle identical to your own, everyone will relate to my writings in a different way. The other day I realized there is one single puzzle piece that we all not only possess, but also find in the center of our puzzles. This critical piece of life is our ability to let go of everything that is not serving us in the best possible manner.

To avoid confusion and misinterpretation, I want it to be understood that in no way shape or form am I implying to disregard your past. Your past has drawn you a general blueprint of how to make the most of your life. This blueprint includes warning-signals of situations you should avoid, and encouragement towards other situations which would behoove you to go after. On that note one can believe that reminiscing in good memories can promote a happy life, just as recalling painful memories can do the opposite. Whether we believe it or not, most of the things that we allow to influence and affect our lives are irrelevant. The only thing that is relevant is our ability to let go of what holds us back. The trick is to breakdown, understand and be selective of the experiences we deem worthy of holding onto. Although our past has put us where we are today, it should never determine our happiness, what we can do, or where go tomorrow.

The idea of letting go is the basis behind every successful form of therapy, self-help, growth and advancement. Regardless of their vast differences, all of these memories have one thing in common; when over-focused on on they can only slow you down and hold back your potential. The whole idea here is to wipe your slate clean before attempting to build anything on top of it. Similar to building a house, without a solid foundation a home is destined to crumble. Regardless of the amount of time or energy that goes into improving or upgrading any other facet of it, the home will be worthless without a solid foundation

We all know someone whose quality of life has been sorely & unjustly impaired by an event in their past. Those who have experienced failure or loss can become inhibited by insecurities that compliment their negative self-image. A self-image that causes them to label themselves as a failure for years to come. Just as easily others can achieve a great accomplishment and become arrogant, self-righteous, or sometimes complacent. Either way, defining yourself based on past events will suffocate your future.

## The Power of Closure

Closure doesn't just apply to situations which have come to an end, I believe it applies to every scenario in which you improve yourself by letting go of something that is holding you back. It can be as simple as understanding the reasons why we made a mistake, or as difficult as weeping over a loved ones grave. It is only possible to gain closure by making peace with reality & letting go of your pain.

Closure is as powerful as it is elusive. By far one of the most difficult and painful things that I have ever had to do was break-up with an absolutely amazing girl that I was dating. Without going into specifics, I can say for certain that she is one of the best people that I will ever be blessed enough to have had in my life. Needless to say I was devastated after breaking up with her. She didn't deserve to be hurt, and there's no one but myself to blame for her tears. It was a reality that made me nauseous from morning to night. I would have literally done anything to take away her pain; instead I beat myself up with blame and felt like a horrible person.

During this time it felt like there was nothing I could do to forgive myself. Time certainly helps to ease the pain of wounds, but no matter how much time has passed you can never fully heal until you find closure. In my case, I voluntarily wore a painful badge of shame for what felt like a lifetime. Even after enough time passed, I was still subconsciously suffering from what felt like a scar left within me. Sometimes it takes more than just time to cure a wound, on occasion it requires a single moment of clarity to find closure and put an end to your distress.

For me, it took the most beautiful and peaceful moment of my life to find the closure I needed. I was happily sitting by myself on the beach of Rio De Janeiro just moments before the start of sunrise. The sun was just starting to peak its brilliant head over the oceans edge, amazing colors were pouring off of the horizon, the warm breeze flowed over me and the soothing sound of crashing waves brought me to an inner calm that I can't translate into words. I didn't have a single care or worry in the world, and in this moment I embraced the re-emergence of my suppressed scar. Seeing this scar in a whole new light, I realized I had to clear my conscience and share with her everything that she deserved to hear (even after all this time). It turned out to be one of the most challenging and eye opening experiences of my life.

## Acknowledge

We are all light-years away from being even close to perfect, and anyone who thinks otherwise is a fool. The fact is we all will undoubtedly fail more times than we'd hope not to. We also cannot avoid the suffering and pain that will come from our experiences. These are passages of life, and while we can acknowledge the past, we should embrace the belief that yesterday should not impact tomorrow.

An extreme example would be how we deal with pain that comes from the loss a loved one. Some are never able to emotionally or psychologically let go of a loved one who has passed. This inability forces the them to choose a life of constant misery and loneliness. The act of mourning is obviously required for any healthy individual to manage their pain, but we can't allow this pain to dwell inside us for too long. Suppressing our emotions is a recipe for prolonged suffering. We should embrace the pain and open ourselves up in order to get it out and move on with our lives. Just as our bodies recognize the need to throw up when we consume excess alcohol, we need to acknowledge & cleanse ourselves of pain and regrets that are poisoning our minds and emotions. I know that when I die, the last thing I want is for my loved ones to suffer. I want each and everyone I leave behind to move on and live happy, fulfilling lives.

Professional athletes are great examples of individuals who's careers hinge on the ability to acknowledge and confront their past. Not only are athletes blessed with superior physical talent, they posses amazing mental and emotional strength. Baseball players for instance typically have a batting average of .266, which roughly means that they will reach base only one out of every four attempts. Needless to say, baseball players must fully acknowledge that they might walk out of the batters box a loser four times more than they will as a winner. Sometimes a failed attempt will be insignificant, other times the odds of inevitable failure will cash in its' ticket during an important inning or defining moment. Players acknowledge that no matter the talent or effort, there will always be moments of disappointment. Just like in anything else, your past only determines your future if you allow it to. Having a clear understanding of this enables you to succeed in the wake of failure.

"I have missed more than 9,000 shots in my career. I have lost almost 300 games, and on 26 occasions I have been entrusted to take the game winning shot, and I missed. I have failed over and over again in my life, and that is why I succeed."

—Michael Jordan—

## Appraise

When appraising a situation, we logically weigh its value and relevance against the benefits as to why "letting go" of it is so vital. In any healthy relationship (romantic, platonic, family, friends etc) there must be a mutual understanding that both parties have nothing but the best of intentions for each other. It is this understanding and trust that enables relationships to recover from conflicts and set backs. Most relationships will face some form of friction at one time or another; there might even be a period where the relationship is tarnished. During these times it must be remembered that we believe the relationship to be valuable and therefore worthy of being reconciled. Of course there will be unavoidable instances where hurtful things will be done or said, what you can avoid is wasting time and energy holding on to these past differences. If a relationship is appraised as being worthy of salvaging, then it is necessary to let go of everything and anything that would restrict it from unconditionally recovering and thriving.

Always remember that you can never properly let go of a grudge or conflict without believing both parties did not intentionally want to cause each other arm. Sometimes you need to assess and confront the emotional predispositions an experience has bestowed upon your psyche. Other times you might accept the fact the relationship is beyond repair, and the other party no longer deserves to be in your life.

One of my good friends (we'll call her Jill) broke up with her boyfriend after making the heartbreaking discovery that he was cheating on her. Jill was mentally and emotionally crushed by the situation, and it understandably took her some time to heal. When Jill started to date new men, she found that it was near impossible to be as vulnerable as before. Jill had unknowingly grown a deep rooted fear of re-experiencing the pain of betrayal. To protect herself, Jill avoided any and all possibilities of being hurt again. For a few years Jill suffered from anxiety and paranoia that she was being lied to & manipulated. The constant stress & worry made Jill say and do stupid things in an effort to keep her worst fears from coming to fruition.

It was no mystery that Jill's trust-issues were the main cause of her pushing new love interests away. Yet she couldn't bring herself to move on from that painful memory and bring her guard down for another. Even when dating a genuinely nice guy, she would sabotage the relationship just to ensure that she wasn't enabling herself to become vulnerable and hurt again. I was always reminding her that her ex-boyfriend was a piece of shit, but no matter how much she agreed, Jill would continue to feel insufficient and self-conscious. Jill constantly felt alone, ashamed and threw away so many opportunities.

One day Jill was flying to California to visit her family & was fortunate enough to have a seat on the plane next to a friendly older woman. Jill and this woman quickly became friends and traded stories during their four hour flight. The woman shared a story of how she fully recovered after her ex-husband left her for another girl shortly after giving birth to their first child. I don't know the specifics of the story, and I guess it doesn't matter; what matters is that Jill related to this story, and was able to finally see the truth behind her own situation. The truth was that there was never anything wrong with Jill (which is the truth because she is awesome). In fact, it was the exposed flaws of her ex-boyfriend that ultimately led to their breakup. The betrayal ended the relationship, and that experience had made Jill a stronger & wiser person today. In seeing this for the first time, Jill understood that it was a blessing the relationship ended how and when it did. Jill will forever credit the older woman's story of self-realization and perseverance to her own epiphany. To this day, Jill and her new friend talk on the phone at least once a week.

## Forgiveness

*"To forgive is to set a prisoner free and discover that prisoner was you."*
—Lewis B. Smedes—

In terms of forgiving, there is nothing more important than creating & maintaining inner-peace. Inner peace can never be realized until you have forgiven yourself for everything in your past. Some will spend their entire life praying for forgiveness. Ironically, we can never receive forgiveness until we forgive ourselves.

Being that we can't forget our past, this makes the task of forgiving difficult. If our experiences created who we are today, then the act of forgetting might also take away our identity. Perhaps we should instead focus on remembering & learning from it. Embrace forgiveness in order to squash a grudge and snuff out resentment between yourself and another. Forgiveness not only sets you free, but allows you to drop the excess negative weight, restricting your ability to find peace within.

## Scrolls

*A midst his various writings and documents, one that stood out was titled Scrolls. After researching, we found this actually came from a book called "The Greatest Salesman in the World", written by Og Mandino.*

*In addition to everything, he especially was a salesman at heart with the gift of persuasion.*

*These 10 scrolls serve as an ode to his spirit and way of life:*

**1. Today I start my new life.** I will shed my old skin which hath, too long suffered the bruises of failure and the wounds of mediocrity. Today I will taste the grapes from these vines and verily I will swallow the seed of success buried in each and new life will sprout within me. The career I have chosen is laden with opportunity yet it is fraught with heartbreak and despair and the bodies of those who have failed are piled on top of each other so high that it would cast a shadow upon all the pyramids on earth. Yet I will not fail like the others before me. Failure will no longer be my payment for struggle. Just as nature made no provision for my body to tolerate pain neither has it made any provision for my life to suffer failure. Failure, like pain, is alien to my life. I will form good habits and become their slave.

**2. I will greet this day with love in my heart.** For this is the greatest success in all ventures of life. Muscle can split a shield, but only the unseen power of love can open the hearts of men, and until I can master this art I will remain no more than a peddler in the market place. I will make love my greatest weapon and none on whom I call can defend against its force. I will greet this day with love in my heart, and how will I do this? I will look at all things with love and I will be born again. I will acknowledge rewards for they are my due, yet I will welcome obstacles for they are my challenge. I will love my enemies and they will become my friends, and I will love my friends whom will become my brothers. Adversity and discouragement will beat against my shield of love and become as soft as rain. I will address those whom I meet with love shining through my eyes, bring a smile to my face and echo it through my voice. I will great this day with love in my heart. Henceforth, I will love all mankind, because there is no time to allow hatred to flow through my veins.

**3. I will persist until I succeed.** I was not delivered into this world in defeat nor does failure course through my veins. Failure I may still encounter at the thousands step, yet success hides behind the next bend in the road. Never will I know how close it lies unless I turn the corner. I will persist until I succeed. I will never consider defeat and I will remove from my vocabulary such terms as "quit, cannot, failure, unworkable, hopeless and retreat". I will ignore the obstacles at my feet and keep my eyes on the goals above my head, for I know where desert dry ends, green grass grows. I will always remember the ancient law of averages and will bend it to my good. I will persist with knowledge that each failure to seed will increase my chance for success at the next attempt. When my thoughts beckon my weak body to go home, I will attempt one more attempt at success. If I persist for long enough, I will inevitably win. I will persist until I succeed.

**4. I am natures greatest miracle.** Only a small portion of my brain do I employ, only a small portion of muscle do I flex. A hundredfold or more can I increase my accomplishments of yesterday and this I will do, starting today. No one has the ability to sell as I can. I am natures greatest miracle, and nature knows no defeat.

**5. I will live this day as if it were my last.** I will spend not a moment dwelling on yesterdays misfortunes, nor will I think of tomorrow. This day is all I have, and these moments are my eternity. I will give great thanks for today as I consider all those who greeted yesterdays sunrise and are no longer with the living today. I have but one life and life is nothing but a measurement of time. If I waste today, I essentially waste the last page of my life. I will live this day as if it were my last. Each minute of this day I will I grasp with both hands and fondle for it is beyond value. A dying man would pay endless fortune for just another breath, what price do I dare place on the hours ahead? I will live this day as if it were my last, and if it is to be my last it will be my greatest moment which I will hold no regrets and hold nothing back.

**6. Today I will be the mast of my emotions.** Yesterdays joy will be today's sadness, and yesterdays will be today's triumph. If my mood is not right, today will be a failure. If I bring my negativity and gloom to my clients, they will surely not purchase my goods. Just as if I bring joy, happiness and comfort to my clients they will surely give me business. Weak is he who allows his thoughts to control his actions, strong is he who forces his actions to dictate his emotions. For this moment I am prepared to control whatever personality awakes in me each day. I will master my moods through positive action, for when I master my moods I will control my destiny. Today I control my destiny and my destiny is to be the greatest sales person in the world

**7. I will laugh at the world.** Humans are the only living beings that have the ability to laugh, and I will cultivate this great gift into habit which will radiate positivity. I will smile to improve my mood and elevate my struggles. Will my concern for today seem silly in future times? I will not submit to petty happenings of today and let them disrupt my humor. Laughter is one of natures greatest gifts, and when unfortunate things occur, I will always remind myself that this will pass. I will laugh at the world. I will remain to busy to be sad, because laughing at the world will make all problems seem tiny. A smile is exchanged for gold, and a frown is exchanged for failure. I will laugh at the world. I will be happy, I will be successful, I will be the worlds greatest salesman.

**8. Today I will multiply my wealth.** The winds will carry my words to those who will listen and announce my goals. I will never set my sights too low, I will do the work that a failure will not do, I will always let my reach exceed my grasps, and I will never be content with my success in the market. Today I will multiply my wealth a hundredfold, and when today is done I will surely do it again. For I am natures greatest gift

**9. I will act now.** Never has a map carried its holder an inch of ground. Action alone is the tinder that ignites the map, opens my dreams, and makes my goals a reality. Action is the food and drink that will forever nourish my success. I will act now. My procrastination which has held me back was born of fear, and now I recognize this secret mined from the depths of all courageous hearts. Now I know that to conquer fear I must always act without hesitation and the flutters in my heart will vanish. Now I know that action reduces the lion of terror to an ant of equanimity. I will act now. I will act now. I will act now. I can condition my mind to perform every act necessary for my success. When I face temptation I will immediately act to remove myself from evil. When I am tempted to quit and begin again tomorrow I will immediately act to consummate another sale. I will act now. Success will not wait, if I delay I will lose the opportunity in which will never be replaced. This is the place, today is the day. I am the man. I will act now.

**10. I will pray.** My cries for help will be nothing more than prayers for guidance. Oh creator of all things, help me. For this day I go out into the world naked and alone, and without your hand to guide me I will wander far from the path which leads to success and happiness. Help me remain humble through obstacles and failures; yet hide not from my eyes the prize that will come with victory. Guide me in my words that they may bear fruit; yet silence me from gossip that none be maligned. Expose me to hate so it not be a stranger; yet fill my cup with love to turn strangers into friends. Let me become all you planned for me when my seed was planted and selected by you to sprout in the vineyard of the world.

# References

**The Beginning**

- Aristotle (attributed). "Knowing yourself is the beginning of all wisdom." Widely quoted, origin uncertain.

**Friends**

- Dhliwayo, Matshona. 100 Lessons I Wish I Learned Sooner. Matshona Dhliwayo, 2016.
  Family

- Peterson, Jordan B. 12 Rules for Life: An Antidote to Chaos. Penguin Random House, 2018.

- Schiller, Johann Christoph Friedrich von. Letters Upon the Aesthetic Education of Man. Translated by John Weiss, Harvard University Press, 1845.

**The Chase**

- Bennington, Chester, et al. "Waiting for the End." A Thousand

Suns, Warner Bros. Records, 2010.

## The Mind

- Koob, George F., et al. Neurobiology of Addiction. Elsevier, 2014.

- Kabat-Zinn, Jon. Wherever You Go, There You Are: Mindfulness Meditation in Everyday Life. Hachette Books, 1994.

- Frankl, Viktor E. Man's Search for Meaning. Beacon Press, 1946.
  A Way Out

- Strayed, Cheryl. Tiny Beautiful Things: Advice on Love and Life from Dear Sugar. Vintage Books, 2012.

- Goggins, David. Can't Hurt Me: Master Your Mind and Defy the Odds. Lioncrest Publishing, 2018.

- Rowling, J.K. Very Good Lives: The Fringe Benefits of Failure and the Importance of Imagination. Little, Brown and Company, 2015.

- von Franz, Marie-Louise. Man and His Symbols. Edited by Carl Jung, Dell Publishing, 1964.

- Carrey, Jim. "Commencement Speech at Maharishi International University." Maharishi International University, May 24, 2014.

## The End

- Robbins, Tony. Awaken the Giant Within: How to Take Immediate Control of Your Mental, Emotional, Physical and Financial Destiny!. Simon & Schuster, 1991.

- Emerson, Ralph Waldo. Essays and Lectures. Edited by Joel Porte, Library of America, 1983.

## The Aftermath

- National Institute on Drug Abuse (NIDA). "Understanding Drug Use and Addiction."

- Miller, William R., and Stephen Rollnick. Motivational Interviewing: Helping People Change. 3rd ed., The Guilford Press, 2013.

- William, Anthony. Medical Medium: Liver Rescue. Hay House, 2018. (For references to liver detox and celery juice.)

- Substance Abuse and Mental Health Services Administration (SAMHSA). "Post-Acute Withdrawal Syndrome and Addiction Recovery."

- Maharishi Foundation. "Transcendental Meditation: Benefits and Practices."

- You Rock Foundation. "Using Music to Combat Depression and Anxiety." Interviews with Corey Taylor and Jonathan Davis. Accessed [URL].

- Sapolsky, Robert M. Why Zebras Don't Get Ulcers.  Holt Paperbacks, 2004. (Insight into stress and nervous system impacts.)

**Recovery**

- Monroe, Robert A. Journeys Out of the Body. Doubleday, 1971. (Verify for the quote, "There is no greater, there is no lesser. There is only balance.")

- van der Kolk, Bessel. The Body Keeps the Score: Brain, Mind, and Body in the Healing of Trauma. Penguin Books, 2015.

- Kübler-Ross, Elisabeth, and David Kessler.  On Grief and Grieving: Finding the Meaning of Grief Through the Five Stages of Loss. Scribner, 2005.

**The Optimist**

- Mandino, Og. The Greatest Salesman in the World. Bantam Books, 1968. (Reference for the 10 scrolls included in the text.)

- Smedes, Lewis B. Forgive and Forget: Healing the Hurts We Don't Deserve. HarperOne, 1984. (For the quote, "To forgive is to set a prisoner free and discover that the prisoner was you.")

- Jordan, Michael. Driven from Within. Atria Books, 2005. (For the quote on failure and success.)

# About the Author

Brandon grew up in the close-knit suburbs of Northern New Jersey, a warm and private community that, like so many others, wasn't untouched by the realities of drug use. From an early age, he found a passion for writing and other creative pursuits, which became outlets for his thoughts and experiences.

Addiction became a part of his life at the age of 20, leading to nearly a decade of challenges. While navigating the darkness of addiction, he also maintained a career in corporate America, often juggling two very different worlds. After losing an early version of Suburban Addict in an unforeseen setback, he faced a profound moment of despair. Following the loss of his father and other personal hardships, Brandon resolved to start over and bring his vision to life again, publishing Suburban Addict two years later.

Through his journey, Brandon has endured many trials but emerged with a clear mission: use his story to inspire others, offer hope, and shed light on the path to recovery. In sharing Suburban Addict, he aims to connect with those in need and remind them that transformation is always possible, no matter how difficult the road may seem.

Contact Information:

**Email**: suburbanaddict1@gmail.com

**Website**: www.suburbanaddict.com

Instagram: @suburbanaddict

www.ingramcontent.com/pod-product-compliance
Lightning Source LLC
Chambersburg PA
CBHW031457120626
46545CB00005B/1643